D1134456

Simple Country Fare

Doreen Fulleylove

Spring Books
London · New York · Sydney · Toronto

Cover photograph by Martin Brigdale
Line drawings by Richard Osborne

First published in
the *Leisure-Plan* series in 1970 by
The Hamlyn Publishing Group Limited
Second edition published in 1974

This edition published in 1983 by
Spring Books
Astronaut House, Feltham, Middlesex, England

ISBN 0 600 38529 9

Printed in Hong Kong

Contents

Introduction

There is still great pleasure and satisfaction in cooking in 'the good old country way' using the bounty of farm, garden and orchard, sea and river as our raw material.

But why should I be writing a book on traditional country fare? For more years than I care to remember I have been a cookery writer for national magazines. In the course of my work I have travelled all over the country meeting housewives and collecting their special recipes and cookery ideas. Whether in remote Scottish croft, Welsh hill farm or on a modern housing estate I have everywhere met pride in the craft of cooking and a long tradition of know-how stretching back from daughter to mother to the days of rural England.

So the purpose of this book is to record some of the great recipes that have fortified and delighted our forebears, as well as including the modern country housewife's contribution.

The big farm kitchen where I am working probably hasn't changed much since the time of Charles II and Samuel Pepys. The beams are dark, the great open fireplace is blackened by the smoke of centuries of fires and the Kentish hills still make the same lovely picture through the leaded lights of the windows.

For centuries in this room great appetites have been appeased, festivals celebrated, marriages cheered, christenings made merry and the rigours of farming comforted by the good fare prepared here. Now it is my family, children and grandchildren who gather here for all family occasions. Perhaps the friendly ghosts of my predecessors have secretly encouraged me to write this book.

Oven Temperatures

Description	Electric Setting	Gas Mark
very cool	225°F–110°C	$\frac{1}{4}$
	250°F–130°C	$\frac{1}{2}$
cool	275°F–140°C	1
	300°F–150°C	2
moderate	325°F–170°C	3
	350°F–180°C	4
moderately hot	375°F–190°C	5
	400°F–200°C	6
hot	425°F–220°C	7
	450°F–230°C	8
very hot	475°F–240°C	9

Note

This table is an approximate guide only. Different makes of cooker vary and if you are in any doubt about the setting it is as well to refer to the manufacturer's temperature chart.

Around Britain Recipes

The astonishing thing about our small country is its infinite variety. Variety of scenery, of people, of culture, of dialect. And so with regional dishes – a strong tradition which is worth trying to preserve against the 'sameness of modern life'.

The very names of these dishes capture the feel of broad acres and sturdy appetites. Here are just a few: Chipstead churdles, Shropshire fitchett pie, Hereford one-pot mince, Wiltshire porkies, Sussex pond pudding, Irish soda bread, Bara brith, Lincolnshire plum bread, Fen Country sweet potato cake. And many, many more. Most are simple to make, all are good to eat.

Savoury Recipes

Yorkshire Bacon and Egg Pie

Cooking time about 1 hour
Oven temperature
400°F., 200°C., Gas Mark 6 for 30 minutes
350°F., 180°C., Gas Mark 4 for 25–30 minutes
Serves 4

Imperial/Metric	American
10 oz./275 g. short crust pastry (see page 44)	10 oz. basic pie dough (see page 44)
for filling	**for filling**
2 tomatoes, sliced	2 tomatoes, sliced
1 tablespoon grated onion	1 tablespoon grated onion
salt and pepper	salt and pepper
8 oz./225 g. lean bacon	½ lb. Canadian bacon
4 medium eggs	4 eggs
for glaze	**for glaze**
beaten egg	beaten egg

Roll out half the pastry into a round and use to line an 8-inch/20-cm. ovenproof pie plate. Trim edges with a knife. Arrange slices of tomato to cover the base. Top with grated onion and seasoning. Trim rind from bacon rashers, chop into small pieces with a knife. Place bacon on top of tomato and onion, leaving four hollows. Carefully break a whole egg into each hollow. Season lightly. Damp edges and place pastry lid in position. Lightly press together and trim away excess pastry. Knock up and flute edges with back of knife. Cut diamond shapes from trimmings and use to decorate pie. Glaze with beaten egg.

Bake on shelf above centre in a hot oven for 30 minutes. Reduce heat to moderate for further 25–30 minutes, or until pastry and filling are cooked through. Serve hot with vegetables or cold with salad.

Buckinghamshire Dumpling

Buckinghamshire Dumpling

Cooking time 2½ hours
Serves 4

Wiltshire Porkies

Cooking time 20 minutes
Serves 4

Imperial/Metric	American
1 lb./450 g. self-raising flour	4 cups all-purpose flour sifted with 4 teaspoons double-acting baking powder
1 level teaspoon salt	1 teaspoon salt
6 oz./175 g. shredded suet	1¼ cups finely chopped beef suet
½ pint/about 3 dl. cold water	1¼ cups cold water
8 oz./225 g. bacon, chopped	½ lb. bacon slices, chopped
8 oz./225 g. liver, chopped	½ lb. liver, chopped
2 large onions, finely chopped	2 large onions, finely chopped
1 level tablespoon dried sage	1 tablespoon dried sage
salt and pepper	salt and pepper
to serve	**to serve**
brown gravy	brown gravy

Sift flour and salt, add suet and mix to a stiff dough with water; roll out on a floured board to a strip 7 inches by 18 inches/18 cm. by 45 cm. Cover dough with chopped bacon, liver, onions, sage and seasoning. Roll up tightly and wrap in well greased foil. Steam for about 2½ hours. Remove foil and serve with brown gravy.

Imperial/Metric	American
4 oz./110 g. plain flour	1 cup all-purpose flour
½ teaspoon salt	½ teaspoon salt
1 egg	1 egg
1 tablespoon cooking oil	1 tablespoon cooking oil
approx. ¼ pint/1½ dl. water	approx. ⅔ cup water
1 lb./450 g. sausage meat	1 lb. sausage meat
2 apples, peeled, cored and cut into rings	2 apples, pared, cored and cut into rings
for frying	**for frying**
deep fat	deep fat

Mix flour and salt in a basin. Separate the egg and add egg yolk, oil and enough water to make a batter which will coat the back of a spoon. With floured hands form sausage meat into small neat rolls. Whisk egg white stiffly and fold into the batter. Coat each roll with batter and fry in deep hot fat for 10–15 minutes until golden brown.

Drain on kitchen paper. Pile on serving dish.

Coat apple rings in remaining batter and deep fry for 5 minutes, drain, then arrange round the 'porkies'.

Wiltshire Fruity Pork Hot-pot

Cooking time 2 hours
Oven temperature
375°F., 190°C., Gas Mark 5
Serves 4

Imperial/Metric	American
4 pork chops	4 pork chops
1 pig's kidney	1 pig kidney
1 tablespoon seasoned flour	1 tablespoon seasoned flour
½ teaspoon mixed herbs	½ teaspoon mixed herbs
1 medium cooking apple	1 medium cooking apple
4 tomatoes	4 tomatoes
8 oz./225 g. onions	½ lb. onions
1–1½ lb./450–675 g. potatoes	1–1½ lb. potatoes
¾ pint/4 dl. perry	1½ cups perry (pear cider)

Trim the meat and kidney, and cut kidney into neat
pieces. Mix the seasoned flour and herbs and use to
coat the meats. Peel, core and slice the apple, skin
tomatoes, leaving them whole. Peel onions and
potatoes then cut into thin slices.

Put into a large casserole or hot-pot dish half the
potatoes, half the onions and half the apple. Add the
chops, kidney and the tomatoes. Cover with
remaining apple, onions and potatoes, in that order.
Sprinkle any remaining seasoned flour on top, and add
extra seasonings to taste. Pour in the perry and cover
with lid.

Cook in moderately hot oven for 2 hours, removing
the lid for the last 15 minutes.

Hereford One-pot Mince

Cooking time about 1 hour
Serves 4

Imperial/Metric	American
1 lb./450 g. minced beef	1 lb. ground beef
1½ oz./40 g. dripping	3 tablespoons drippings
1 oz./25 g. plain flour	¼ cup all-purpose flour
salt and pepper	salt and pepper
¾ pint/4 dl. cider	scant 2 cups cider
4 small onions	4 small onions
4 tomatoes	4 tomatoes
8–12 small potatoes	8–12 small potatoes
for garnish	**for garnish**
chopped parsley	chopped parsley

Fry the mince in a little dripping in a saucepan until
well browned, stirring constantly with a fork. Sprinkle
the flour over the meat and mix in with salt and
pepper. Add the cider and simmer for 5 minutes,
stirring.

Peel the onions, tomatoes and potatoes and place,
whole, in a pan or casserole. Pour in the mince and
cover with a lid. Simmer for about 40 minutes until
vegetables are cooked. Arrange vegetables round edge
of a serving dish and pour mince into centre. Garnish
with chopped parsley.

Lancashire Hot-pot

Cooking time 2½-3 hours
Oven temperature
325°F., 170°C., Gas Mark 3
Serves 4

Imperial/Metric	American
1½ lb./675 g. middle neck	1½ lb. lamb neck slices or
of mutton	shoulder
2 sheep's kidneys (optional)	2 lamb kidneys (optional)
1–1½ lb./450–675 g. potatoes	1–1½ lb. potatoes
2 large onions	2 large onions
salt and pepper	salt and pepper
½ pint/3 dl. stock	1¼ cups stock

Trim the meat and kidneys and cut into neat pieces.
Peel the potatoes thinly and slice. Slice the onions
thinly. Put layers of the meat and vegetables into a
greased casserole. Season each layer well and finish
with a layer of potatoes. Add about ½ pint/3 dl. of
stock or water and cover with casserole lid or
aluminium foil.

Bake in a very moderate oven for about 2½–3 hours,
removing the lid for the last 30 minutes to brown the
potatoes. Add small dabs of dripping or butter if
potatoes get too dry during cooking.

Lancashire Hot-pot

Chipstead Churdles

Chipstead Churdles

Cooking time about 45 minutes
Oven temperature
375°F., 190°C., Gas Mark 5
Makes 6 churdles

Imperial/Metric	American
8 oz./225 g. short crust pastry (see page 44)	½ lb. basic pie dough (see page 44)
for filling	**for filling**
1 onion, chopped	1 onion, chopped
6 oz./175 g. lamb's liver	6 oz. lamb liver
1 oz./25 g. dripping	2 tablespoons drippings
6 oz./175 g. bacon pieces	6 oz. bacon strips
2 oz./50 g. mushrooms, chopped	½ cup chopped mushrooms
1 small cooking apple, chopped	1 small cooking apple, chopped
1 tablespoon chopped parsley	1 tablespoon chopped parsley
salt and pepper	salt and pepper
1 tablespoon browned crumbs	1 tablespoon browned crumbs
1 tablespoon grated cheese	good 1 tablespoon grated cheese
for garnish	**for garnish**
tomato halves	tomato halves
parsley sprigs	parsley sprigs

Lightly fry onion and liver in the dripping for a few minutes, then mince or chop finely with the bacon pieces. Add mushrooms, apple and parsley. Season with salt and pepper.

Roll out pastry on lightly floured board.

With an up-turned saucer as guide, cut six pastry circles. Brush outside edges with water or milk. Divide filling mixture into six and place one portion on each circle. Pinch up edges to make three-cornered hat shape, leaving filling exposed in centre, stand churdles

on a baking sheet. Brush pastry with water or milk. Mix crumbs and cheese and sprinkle over churdles. Bake in a moderately hot oven for 40 minutes or until golden brown. Garnish with tomato halves and parsley.

Shropshire Fitchett Pie

Cooking time 1 hour
Oven temperature
425°F., 220°C., Gas Mark 7 for 10 minutes
375°F., 190°C., Gas Mark 5 for 40 minutes
Serves 4

Imperial/Metric	American
8 oz./225 g. flaky pastry (see page 44)	½ lb. rich flaky pie dough (see page 44)
for filling	**for filling**
1 oz./25 g. cooking fat	2 tablespoons shortening
8 oz./225 g. bacon, coarsely chopped	½ lb. bacon slices, coarsely chopped
8 oz./225 g. onions, peeled and sliced into rings	½ lb. onions, peeled and sliced into rings
1 lb./450 g. cooking apples, peeled, cored and sliced	1 lb. cooking apples, pared, cored and sliced
1 tablespoon black treacle	1 tablespoon molasses
1 tablespoon hot water	1 tablespoon hot water
salt and pepper	salt and pepper

Melt fat in a pan, add bacon and onions and fry gently for about 10 minutes until soft but not crisp. Fill a medium size pie dish with alternate layers of apples and fried bacon and onions, then add treacle mixed with water. Sprinkle lightly with salt and pepper. Damp edges of pie dish with water. Roll out pastry on lightly floured board and cover the pie, trim, rough up and flute edges. Brush with beaten egg and bake in centre of a hot oven for 10 minutes, then turn down oven to moderately hot, bake for another 40 minutes.

Welsh Rarebit

Cooking time about 8 minutes
Serves 4

Imperial/Metric	American
1 oz./25 g. butter	2 tablespoons butter
1 level tablespoon flour	1 tablespoon flour
3 tablespoons milk	4 tablespoons milk
2 tablespoons beer	3 tablespoons beer
1 teaspoon mixed mustard	1 teaspoon prepared mustard
few drops Worcestershire sauce	few drops Worcestershire sauce
4–6 oz./100–175 g. Cheddar cheese, grated	1–1½ cups grated Cheddar cheese
salt and pepper	salt and pepper
4 slices hot buttered toast	4 slices hot buttered toast
for garnish	**for garnish**
few tomato slices	few tomato slices

Melt fat in pan and stir in flour, add milk and continue stirring until mixture forms a thick smooth sauce. Then add the beer, mustard, Worcestershire sauce, cheese and season to taste. Do not overcook the mixture. Spread mixture on buttered toast and put under a hot grill until golden brown. Top each with a tomato slice.

Sweet Recipes

Kent Apple Scone

Cooking time 30 minutes
Oven temperature
400°F., 200°C., Gas Mark 6
Makes 8 wedges

Imperial/Metric	American
2 medium cooking apples	2 medium cooking apples
1 lb./450 g. self-raising flour	4 cups all-purpose flour sifted with 4 teaspoons double-acting baking powder
1 teaspoon salt	1 teaspoon salt
2 level teaspoons baking powder	2 teaspoons double-acting baking powder
4 oz./110 g. butter	½ cup butter
4 oz./110 g. castor sugar	½ cup sugar
scant ½ pint/3 dl. milk	scant 1¼ cups milk
1 tablespoon sieved apricot jam	1–2 tablespoons apricot jelly

Peel, core and finely chop one apple. Sift together the flour, salt and baking powder. Rub in butter, then add castor sugar and chopped apple. Mix to a soft, but not sticky, dough with milk. Roll out to 8-inch/20-cm. circle and place on a floured baking sheet.

Mark top into eight wedges. Peel and core remaining apple and cut into thin slices. Brush top of scone with milk and arrange apple slices on top.

Bake in a hot oven for about 30 minutes. While still hot, brush apple slices with apricot jam. Serve warm with butter.

Norfolk Scone

Norfolk Scone

Cooking time about 50 minutes
Oven temperature
400°F., 200°C., Gas Mark 6
Makes 8 wedges

Imperial/Metric	American
1 lb./450 g. self-raising flour	4 cups all-purpose flour sifted with 4 teaspoons double-acting baking powder
1 teaspoon salt	1 teaspoon salt
4 oz./110 g. butter or margarine	½ cup butter or margarine
2 eggs	2 eggs
¼ pint/1½ dl. milk plus about 4 tablespoons	1 cup milk
for filling	**for filling**
1 oz./25 g. softened butter or margarine	2 tablespoons softened butter or margarine
4 oz./110 g. currants	1 cup currants
½ teaspoon grated nutmeg	½ teaspoon grated nutmeg
4 oz./110 g. demerara sugar	½ cup raw sugar

Sift together the flour and salt. Rub in butter or margarine until mixture resembles fine breadcrumbs. Mix to a soft dough with the eggs and milk beaten together. Turn on to a floured board and knead lightly. Divide in half and roll each out into an 8-inch/20-cm. circle. Lift one circle on to a baking sheet and spread top with the softened butter. Mix currants, nutmeg and 3 oz./75 g. sugar together and sprinkle this mixture over butter. Place second circle on top, mark and cut through into eight wedges. Brush with milk and sprinkle over remaining sugar. Bake in a hot oven for about 50 minutes.

Somerset Apples

Cooking time 35–40 minutes
Oven temperature
375°F., 190°C., Gas Mark 5
Serves 4

Imperial/Metric	American
4 cooking apples	4 cooking apples
1 oz./25 g. butter	2 tablespoons butter
for stuffing	**for stuffing**
4 oz./100 g. seedless raisins	¾ cup seedless raisins
2 oz./50 g. almonds, blanched	½ cup almonds, blanched
2 oz./50 g. demerara sugar	4 tablespoons raw sugar
a few glacé cherries	a few candied cherries
1 oz./25 g. butter	2 tablespoons butter
for glaze	**for glaze**
2 tablespoons redcurrant jelly	2–3 tablespoons red currant jelly
2 tablespoons rose hip syrup	2–3 tablespoons rose hip syrup

Wipe the apples and remove cores, stand them in an ovenproof dish. Mix together raisins, almonds and sugar and stuff apples with this mixture. Arrange cherries on top of apples and place a knob of butter on each. Bake in a moderately hot oven for 35–40 minutes.

Heat the redcurrant jelly and rose hip syrup together and pour over cooked apples.

Shown in colour on page 23

Somerset Bramble and Apple Pie

Cooking time 40 minutes
Oven temperature
375°F., 190°C., Gas Mark 5
Serves 4

Imperial/Metric	American
8 oz./225 g. short crust pastry (see page 44)	½ lb. basic pie dough (see page 44)
beaten egg or milk	beaten egg or milk
for filling	**for filling**
1 lb./450 g. dessert apples	1 lb. dessert apples
1 oz./25 g. sugar	2 tablespoons sugar
juice of 1 lemon	juice of 1 lemon
6 oz./175 g. bramble jelly	½ cup bramble (blackberry) jelly
1 oz./25 g. chopped nuts	¼ cup chopped nuts

Line a shallow pie dish with rolled out pastry, trim and flute edges and bake 'blind' (see page 43) in centre of a moderately hot oven for 25 minutes. Cut fruit-leaf shapes from pastry trimmings, glaze with beaten egg or milk and bake at same time as pie case.

Core and slice apples but do not skin. Place apples, sugar and lemon juice in a pan and cook over low heat for 10 minutes. Add bramble jelly and cook for a further 4 minutes. Allow to cool. Turn apple filling into baked pastry case. Sprinkle with chopped nuts and decorate with pastry fruit leaves.

Shown in colour on page 23

Sussex Pond Pudding

Cooking time 2½–3 hours
Serves 4

Imperial/Metric for suet crust pastry	American for suet crust
8 oz./225 g. self-raising flour	2 cups all-purpose flour sifted with 2 teaspoons double-acting baking powder
1 teaspoon salt	1 teaspoon salt
3 oz./75 g. shredded suet	⅔ cup finely chopped beef suet
2 oz./50 g. castor sugar	4 tablespoons granulated sugar
2 oz./50 g. currants	⅓ cup currants
¼ pint/1½ dl. water (scant measure)	⅔ cup water (scant measure)
for filling	**for filling**
8 oz./225 g. butter	1 cup butter
4 oz./100 g. demerara sugar	½ cup raw sugar

Sieve together the flour and salt. Mix in the suet, sugar and currants, add the water. Mix to a soft dough with a round-bladed knife. Lightly knead on a floured board until pastry is smooth. Divide pastry in half and roll each piece to a 6-inch/15-cm. circle. Blend together butter and demerara sugar and mould into a ball. Put ball in centre of one round. Gather up edges of crust and enclose butter ball, then cover with second circle and pinch edges together. Grease a piece of 18-inches/45-cm. square kitchen foil, tie up pudding tightly and steam for 2½–3 hours.

Devonshire Splits

Cooking time 10–15 minutes
Oven temperature
400°F., 200°C., Gas Mark 6
Makes 24 splits

Imperial/Metric	American
12 oz./350 g. self-raising flour	3 cups all-purpose flour sifted with 3 teaspoons double-acting baking powder
pinch of salt	pinch of salt
4½ oz./125 g. margarine	½ cup plus 1 tablespoon margarine
3 oz./75 g. castor sugar	6 tablespoons granulated sugar
about 4 tablespoons milk	about 5 tablespoons milk
to serve	**to serve**
about 2–3 oz./50–75 g. butter	about 4–6 tablespoons butter
3 tablespoons strawberry jam	¼ cup strawberry jam
4 oz./100 g. Devonshire clotted cream or ¼ pint/1½ dl. whipped double cream	⅔ cup Devonshire clotted cream or ⅔ cup whipped heavy cream

Sift the flour and salt into a bowl, rub in the margarine with the fingertips until mixture resembles fine breadcrumbs. Stir in castor sugar, mix to a stiff dough with the milk. Knead until smooth and free from cracks.

Roll out dough on a lightly floured board to ¾ inch/ 2 cm. thick. Cut into 2½-inch/6-cm. rounds. Place on a greased baking tray and bake on shelf above centre of a hot oven for about 10–15 minutes, until well risen and cooked through. Transfer to a wire rack, allow to cool. Split or cut in half, spread with butter, serve with strawberry jam and clotted or whipped double cream.

Yorkshire Parkin

Cooking time 1½ hours
Oven temperature
275°F., 140°C., Gas Mark 1
Makes 1 parkin

Imperial/Metric	American
4 oz./110 g. plain flour	1 cup all-purpose flour
good pinch of salt	good pinch of salt
1 teaspoon ground ginger	1 teaspoon ground ginger
½ teaspoon nutmeg	½ teaspoon ground nutmeg
4 oz./110 g. soft brown sugar	½ cup brown sugar
12 oz./350 g. oatmeal	2 cups oatmeal
4 oz./110 g. margarine	½ cup margarine
10 oz./275 g. golden syrup	generous ¾ cup corn syrup
½ teaspoon bicarbonate of soda	½ teaspoon baking soda
2 tablespoons milk	3 tablespoons milk

Line the base of an oblong baking pan with kitchen foil. Sift the flour, salt, ginger and nutmeg together into a bowl. Add brown sugar and oatmeal. Heat margarine and syrup gently until the margarine has melted, then stir into dry ingredients and beat well. Dissolve bicarbonate of soda in milk, beat into mixture.

Turn into prepared pan and bake in a cool oven for 1½ hours, or until cooked through. When cold turn on to a wire rack.

Note
Cut into squares. Keep for few days in airtight tin before eating.

North Country Mint Pasties

Cooking time 20 minutes
Oven temperature
400°F., 200°C., Gas Mark 6
Serves 4

Imperial/Metric	American
8 oz./225 g. short crust pastry (see page 44)	½ lb. basic pie dough (see page 44)
for filling	**for filling**
2 oz./50 g. mixed peel	⅓ cup mixed candied peel
2 oz./50 g. currants	⅓ cup currants
2 oz./50 g. demerara sugar	4 tablespoons raw sugar
1 oz./25 g. butter, melted	2 tablespoons melted butter
2 tablespoons fresh mint, finely chopped	2 tablespoons finely chopped fresh mint
for glaze	**for glaze**
milk	milk

Divide the pastry into four and roll each piece to a 6-inch/15-cm. circle. Mix filling ingredients together and divide equally among rounds. Wet pastry edges really well and fold over. Press edges firmly together and crimp with the finger and thumb. Brush with milk and bake in a moderately hot oven for about 20 minutes, until golden brown. Serve hot or cold.

North Country Mint Pasties

Fen Country Sweet Potato Cake

Cooking time about 30 minutes
Oven temperature
375°F., 190°C., Gas Mark 5
Serves 4

Imperial/Metric	American
1 lb./450 g. cooked potatoes	1 lb. boiled potatoes
4 oz./100 g. castor sugar	½ cup granulated sugar
4 oz./100 g. candied peel, finely chopped	⅔ cup finely chopped candied peel
2 oz./50 g. butter, melted	2 tablespoons melted butter
few drops vanilla essence	few drops vanilla extract
2 eggs	2 eggs
castor sugar to sprinkle on top	granulated or powdered sugar to sprinkle on top

Fen Country Sweet Potato Cake

Grease a sandwich tin. Sieve the cooked potatoes into a basin, stir in sugar, peel, butter and essence. Separate the eggs and add beaten yolks to mixture. Fold in the stiffly whisked egg whites. If the mixture appears to be dry, a little milk may be added. Turn mixture into prepared pan, smooth top and bake in a moderately hot oven until nicely browned.
Turn out, sprinkle with sugar and serve very hot.

Scotch Pancakes

Cooking time about 7 minutes
Makes 16 pancakes

Imperial/Metric	American
4 oz./110 g. plain flour	1 cup all-purpose flour
1 level teaspoon cream of tartar	1 teaspoon cream of tartar
½ level teaspoon bicarbonate of soda	½ teaspoon baking soda
good pinch of salt	good pinch of salt
2 tablespoons castor sugar	3 tablespoons granulated sugar
1 egg	1 egg
approx. ¼ pint/1½ dl. milk	approx. ⅔ cup milk

Sift the flour, cream of tartar, bicarbonate of soda and salt together into a mixing bowl. Stir in sugar. Make a well in the centre and drop in the egg with a little of the milk. Mix well, gradually drawing in the flour from the sides of the bowl. Gradually add the remaining milk to make a smooth batter.
Lightly grease a griddle, heavy frying pan or solid electric hot-plate, and place on spoonfuls of the prepared batter. Pour from the tip of the spoon to give a good round shape. Cook until the surface of the scones is full of bubbles and the underside is golden brown. Turn over with a palette knife and cook on the other side. Serve at once with butter, or place between folds of a teatowel until required.

Dundee Cake

Highland Shortbread

Cooking time 1 hour
Oven temperature
300°F., 150°C., Gas Mark 2
Makes 2 rounds

Imperial/Metric	American
12 oz./350 g. plain flour	3 cups all-purpose flour
4 oz./110 g. castor sugar	½ cup granulated sugar
a good pinch of salt	a good pinch of salt
8 oz./225 g. butter	1 cup butter
castor sugar to dredge	granulated or powdered sugar to dredge

Place the flour, sugar and salt on a large board or table surface. (If this is not possible, a bowl may be used.) Make a well in the centre and put in the butter which has been cut into large pieces. Gradually work the dry ingredients into the butter with tips of the fingers to form a smooth paste. Knead lightly, divide into two, roll into rounds ¾ inch/2 cm. thick and transfer to lightly greased baking trays.

Prick surfaces with a fork and pinch up edges. Mark lightly into triangles with a knife and bake on centre shelf of a very cool oven for 1 hour, or until pale golden in colour and cooked through. Transfer to a wire rack and allow to cool. Sprinkle with castor sugar and when cold break into triangles, if liked.

Note
Store in an airtight tin until required.

Dundee Cake

Cooking time 2½–3 hours
Oven temperature
350°F., 180°C., Gas Mark 4 for 1 hour
275°F., 140°C., Gas Mark 1 for 1½–2 hours

Imperial/Metric	American
10 oz./275 g. plain flour	2½ cups all-purpose flour
¼ level teaspoon bicarbonate of soda	¼ teaspoon baking soda
a good pinch of salt	a good pinch of salt
8 oz./225 g. butter	1 cup butter
8 oz./225 g. castor sugar	1 cup granulated sugar
4 eggs	4 eggs
grated rind of 1 orange	grated rind of 1 orange
1 oz./25 g. chopped almonds	¼ cup chopped almonds
8 oz./225 g. sultanas	1¼ cups seedless white raisins
8 oz./225 g. currants	1¼ cups currants
2 oz./50 g. chopped glacé cherries	⅓ cup chopped candied cherries
2 oz./50 g. chopped mixed peel	⅓ cup chopped candied peel
2 oz./50–75 g. split blanched almonds	½–¾ cup split blanched almonds

Line a greased 8-inch/20-cm. round pan with greased greaseproof paper. Sift the flour, bicarbonate of soda and salt together. Cream butter and sugar together until light and fluffy. Lightly whisk the eggs, then beat well into creamed mixture, a little at a time, with a little of the sifted flour, if necessary, to prevent curdling. Stir in grated orange rind and fold in remaining flour. Carefully stir in chopped almonds, sultanas, currants, cherries and mixed peel until thoroughly mixed.

Turn into the prepared pan and smooth top of the mixture with a palette knife. Make a shallow dip in the centre of the cake and lay the split almonds on top in a neat design.

Cook towards centre of a moderate oven for approximately 1 hour, then reduce oven temperature to cool for about 1½–2 hours, or until cake is well risen and cooked through – test with a skewer. It may be necessary to cover the top of the cake after 2 hours to prevent it from over-browning.

Note
This cake will keep well in an airtight tin for up to two weeks before cutting.

Irish Soda Bread

Cooking time 35–45 minutes
Oven temperature
425°F., 220°C., Gas Mark 7
Makes a 1½-lb./675-g. loaf

Imperial/Metric	American
1 lb./450 g. plain flour	4 cups all-purpose flour
1 level teaspoon salt	1 teaspoon salt
2 level teaspoons bicarbonate of soda	2 teaspoons baking soda
½–¾ pint/3–4 dl. sour milk or buttermilk	1¼–scant 2 cups sour milk or buttermilk

Sift the flour, salt and bicarbonate of soda into a bowl. Make a well in the centre and pour in a generous ½ pint/3 dl. of sour milk or buttermilk. Mix with a knife to a soft dough. If the dough seems a little dry, cut in a little more liquid through the centre of the dough using a knife.

Knead lightly with the fingertips to a round shape. Turn smooth-side up, place on a floured baking tray and cut a deep cross on top to allow the bread to rise evenly.

Bake on shelf above centre in a hot oven for 35–45 minutes until well risen and lightly brown. When cooked, the loaf should sound hollow if tapped on base. Cool on a wire tray.

Lincolnshire Plum Bread

Lincolnshire Plum Bread

Cooking time 3 hours
Oven temperature
250°F., 130°C., Gas Mark ½
Makes 1 loaf

Imperial/Metric	American
4 oz./110 g. butter	1 cup butter
4 oz./110 g. demerara sugar	½ cup raw sugar
¾ teaspoon powdered cinnamon	¾ teaspoon powdered cinnamon
½ teaspoon mixed spice	½ teaspoon mixed spice
½ teaspoon liquid gravy browning	½ teaspoon liquid gravy coloring
2 eggs	2 eggs
1 tablespoon brandy	1 tablespoon brandy
7 oz./200 g. self-raising flour	1¾ cups all-purpose flour sifted with 2 teaspoons double-acting baking powder
pinch of salt	pinch of salt
4 oz./110 g. prunes, steeped for 2 days in cold water and finely chopped	⅔ cup prunes, steeped for 2 days in cold water and finely chopped
4 oz./110 g. currants	⅔ cup currants
4 oz./110 g. sultanas	⅔ cup seedless white raisins

Grease and line a 2-lb./1-kg. loaf pan. Cream the fat and sugar together until light and fluffy, beat in spices, browning, eggs and brandy gradually. Sift in flour and salt. Stir in prepared fruit. Turn into prepared pan and bake in very cool oven for about 3 hours, or until cooked through.

Turn out and cool on a wire rack.

Bara Brith (Welsh Bun Loaf)

Cooking time 1–1¼ hours
Oven temperature
375°F., 190°C., Gas Mark 5
Makes 1 loaf

Imperial/Metric	American
1 lb./450 g. plain flour	4 cups all-purpose flour
½ level teaspoon salt	½ teaspoon salt
3 oz./75 g. butter or margarine	6 tablespoons butter or margarine
4 oz./110 g. sugar	½ cup granulated sugar
6 oz./175 g. mixed dried fruit	1 cup mixed dried fruit
½ oz./15 g. dried yeast	2 packages active dry yeast
¼ pint/1½ dl. warm water	⅔ cup warm water
¼ pint/1½ dl. warm milk	⅔ cup warm milk

Sift the flour and salt into a bowl. Rub in the fat lightly. Mix in all but 1 teaspoon of sugar and cleaned dried fruit. Place yeast, rest of sugar and warm water in a jug and stand in a warm place until frothy on top, about 10 minutes. Add to flour mixture together with warm milk to make a soft dough. Knead for a few minutes then cover bowl and leave in a warm place until dough is doubled in size, about 1½ hours, and springs back when pressed with floured finger. Turn on to a lightly floured board and knead for about 10 minutes.

Shape dough and place in lightly greased 2-lb./1-kg. loaf pan. Cover pan and leave in a warm place to rise for about 30 minutes. Bake just below centre in a moderately hot oven for 1–1¼ hours until well browned and loaf sounds hollow when tapped. Serve thinly sliced, spread with butter.

One of the most traditional meals in all the land is the ploughman's lunch: a hearty chunk of good farmhouse cheese with crusty bread. And if you have a bowl of new-laid eggs and fresh salad ingredients you lack nothing for a feast. An appetite keened by fresh air can be deliciously satisfied by this simple fare.

Egg, Cheese and Salad Dishes

Egg Dishes

Farmer's Omelette

Cooking time about 20 minutes
Serves 1

Imperial/Metric	American
1 large raw potato	1 large raw potato
1 oz./25 g. butter	2 tablespoons butter
2 oz./50 g. Cheddar cheese	½ cup finely diced Cheddar cheese
2 eggs	2 eggs
salt and pepper	salt and pepper
a few chopped chives	a few chopped chives

Peel the potato and cut into very small dice. Melt the butter in an omelette pan and cook potato, shaking often until golden brown and crisp all over. Add cheese cut into small dice. Pour the lightly beaten, well seasoned eggs over potato and cheese and cook until almost set. Place under a hot grill for 2–3 minutes to set the top, then transfer to a serving dish and sprinkle with a few chopped chives.

Variations
Add 1 small onion, finely chopped, to potato.

Add sprinkling of dried mixed herbs to potato and cheese mixture.

Fried Bacon and Egg Fingers

Cooking time about 10 minutes
Serves 4

Imperial/Metric	American
8 bacon rashers	8 bacon slices
2 eggs	2 eggs
salt and pepper	salt and pepper
2 thick slices white bread	2 thick slices white bread

Fry the bacon, adding a little extra fat to the pan if necessary. Beat the eggs well and season. Cut the bread into fingers and dip in egg until soaked through. Fry in hot bacon fat until crisp and golden on both sides. Serve with the bacon.

Eggs Victoriana

Cooking time about 30 minutes
Oven temperature
425°F., 220°C., Gas Mark 7
Serves 4

Imperial/Metric	American
4 hard-boiled eggs, sliced	4 hard-cooked eggs, sliced
1 oz./25 g. butter	2 tablespoons butter
1 large onion, finely sliced	1 large onion, finely sliced
1 oz./25 g. plain flour	¼ cup all-purpose flour
¾ pint/4 dl. milk	scant 2 cups milk
salt and pepper	salt and pepper
4–6 oz./100–175 g. Cheddar cheese, grated	1–1½ cups grated Cheddar cheese

Arrange the hard-boiled eggs in base of a shallow ovenproof dish. Keep warm. Melt the butter in a saucepan, add onion, and fry gently until completely tender, but not browned. Stir in the flour and cook for a minute. Remove from heat and stir in milk gradually. Return to heat and bring to the boil, stirring. Cook for a minute, season, and pour over eggs in dish. Sprinkle cheese over top, and place in a hot oven for about 20 minutes to brown.

Scotch Eggs

Cooking time about 5 minutes
Serves 4

Imperial/Metric	American
4 hard-boiled eggs	4 hard-cooked eggs
1 tablespoon seasoned flour	1 tablespoon seasoned flour
few drops Worcestershire or other piquant sauce	few drops Worcestershire or other piquant sauce
8 oz./225 g. sausage meat	½ lb. (1 cup) sausage meat
1 egg	1 egg
fresh breadcrumbs	fresh bread crumbs
fat for deep frying	fat for deep frying

Shell the eggs, dip in seasoned flour. Add a few drops of Worcestershire or other sauce to the sausage meat and mix well together.

Divide into four and cover each egg completely with the mixture. Coat in beaten egg and breadcrumbs. Fry in deep hot fat until golden brown all over, giving enough cooking time to cook the sausage meat right through (about 5 minutes). Drain well on kitchen paper. Cut in half lengthwise, and serve hot with tomato sauce and vegetables or cold with salad.

Shirred Eggs

Cooking time about 10 minutes
Oven temperature
350°F., 180°C., Gas Mark 4
Serves 4

Imperial/Metric	American
2 oz./50 g. butter	¼ cup butter
4 eggs	4 eggs
salt and pepper	salt and pepper
for garnish	**for garnish**
parsley sprigs	parsley sprigs

Divide the butter equally between four small fireproof dishes. Heat until butter bubbles. Break each egg into a cup, then transfer to a dish. Sprinkle with salt and pepper and bake in a moderate oven for 10 minutes, or until whites of eggs are set. Garnish with a sprig of parsley on each.

Egg and Fish Scramble

Cooking time about 3 minutes
Serves 4

Imperial/Metric	American
4 oz./100 g. boned cooked fish (any white fish, smoked haddock or kipper)	¼ lb. boned cooked fish (any white fish, smoked haddock or kipper)
3 eggs	3 eggs
1 tablespoon milk	good tablespoon milk
pinch of dry mustard	pinch of dry mustard
salt and pepper	salt and pepper
1 oz./25 g. butter	2 tablespoons butter
4 rounds buttered toast	4 slices buttered toast
for garnish	**for garnish**
a little chopped parsley	a little chopped parsley

Flake the fish finely. Whisk the eggs, milk and seasonings together then stir in prepared fish. Melt the butter in a saucepan. Pour in mixture and stir continually until lightly scrambled. Pile on to rounds of buttered toast and sprinkle top with a little parsley.

Hopel Popel

Cooking time about 10 minutes
Serves 4

Imperial/Metric	American
2 oz./50 g. butter	¼ cup butter
4 oz./100 g. streaky bacon, diced	¼ lb. diced bacon slices
1 onion, finely chopped	1 onion, finely chopped
4 oz./100 g. mushrooms, chopped	1 cup chopped mushrooms
1 lb./450 g. boiled potatoes, diced	1 lb. boiled potatoes, diced
4 eggs	4 eggs
salt and pepper	salt and pepper
2 oz./50 g. Cheddar cheese, grated	½ cup grated Cheddar cheese

Melt the butter in a frying pan, add the bacon, onion and mushrooms, fry gently for a few minutes until tender. Add the potatoes and allow to warm through. Beat the eggs with seasoning and pour over mixture, sprinkle with grated cheese and cook slowly until the eggs are set. Brown the top under grill for a minute or two. Serve hot cut in wedges.

Baked Egg Custard

Cooking time 30–40 minutes
Oven temperature
300°F., 150°C., Gas Mark 2
Serves 4

Imperial/Metric	American
2 eggs	2 eggs
1 oz./25 g. castor sugar	2 tablespoons granulated sugar
1 pint/6 dl. milk	2½ cups milk
a little grated nutmeg	a little grated nutmeg

Beat the eggs and sugar lightly. Add the milk and mix well until the sugar is dissolved. Strain into a greased pie dish. Grate a little nutmeg over the top. Bake in the middle of a slow oven for 30–40 minutes.

Quick Salad Dressing

Imperial/Metric	American
4 tablespoons olive oil	5 tablespoons olive oil
2 tablespoons wine vinegar	3 tablespoons wine vinegar
¼ level teaspoon each : dry mustard, salt, sugar and pepper	¼ teaspoon each : dry mustard, salt, sugar and pepper
2–3 hard-boiled eggs	2–3 hard-cooked eggs
1 tablespoon chopped parsley	1 tablespoon chopped parsley

Place oil, vinegar, mustard, salt, sugar and pepper in a screw-topped jar and shake until thoroughly blended. Shell and finely chop the eggs, then stir into the dressing together with the parsley just before serving. Serve with cold meat or fish salads.

Egg Sauce

Imperial/Metric	American
½ oz./15 g. butter or margarine	1 tablespoon butter or margarine
½ oz./15 g. plain flour	2 tablespoons all-purpose flour
½ pint/3 dl. milk	1¼ cups milk
a small pinch of cayenne pepper	a small pinch of cayenne
salt	salt
2–3 hard-boiled eggs	2–3 hard-cooked eggs

Melt the fat in a small pan and stir in the flour. Gradually blend in the milk to make a smooth sauce. Add a pinch of cayenne and salt to taste. Bring to the boil, still stirring, and cook for 3 minutes. Shell and chop the eggs. Mix into the sauce and heat for a few seconds. Can be served with ham, bacon or fish dishes.

Mayonnaise

Makes ¼ pint (1½ dl.)

Imperial/Metric	American
1 egg yolk	1 egg yolk
¼ level teaspoon each : salt, pepper and dry mustard	¼ teaspoon each : salt, pepper and dry mustard
1 level teaspoon castor sugar	1 teaspoon granulated sugar
1 tablespoon tarragon vinegar or lemon juice	1 tablespoon tarragon vinegar or lemon juice
¼ pint/1½ dl. olive oil or corn oil	⅔ cup olive oil or corn oil

Mix the egg yolk, seasonings and sugar together in a bowl. Stir in 1 teaspoon vinegar, or lemon juice, and whisk. Add half the oil drop by drop, whisking well after each addition. Add remaining oil in a thin stream, whisking all the time until the mixture is thick and creamy. Gradually stir in the remaining vinegar or lemon juice.

Note

2 tablespoons whipped cream may be added, if liked.

Cheese Dishes

Creamy Cheese and Onion Soup

Cooking time about 15 minutes
Serves 4

Imperial/Metric	American
1 oz./25 g. butter	2 tablespoons butter
1 lb./450 g. onions, thinly sliced	1 lb. onions, thinly sliced
1 oz./25 g. plain flour	¼ cup all-purpose flour
1 pint/6 dl. milk	2½ cups milk
¾ pint/4 dl. water	scant 2 cups water
salt and pepper	salt and pepper
6 oz./175 g. Cheddar cheese, grated	1½ cups grated Cheddar cheese
for garnish	**for garnish**
chopped parsley	chopped parsley

Melt the butter in a large saucepan. Add onions and gently fry until tender but not browned, about 10 minutes. Add the flour and cook for a minute, stirring. Gradually stir in milk and water and bring to the boil. Season, and cook for 2 minutes. Remove from the heat, stir in cheese until it has melted. Garnish with chopped parsley to serve.

Cheese and Shrimp Soup

Cooking time about 10–15 minutes
Serves 4

Imperial/Metric	American
1 large onion, finely chopped	1 large onion, finely chopped
2 oz./50 g. butter	¼ cup butter
1 oz./25 g. flour	¼ cup flour
1 pint/6 dl. milk	2½ cups milk
1 pint/6 dl. stock	2½ cups stock
salt and pepper	salt and pepper
dry mustard	dry mustard
1 teaspoon lemon juice	1 teaspoon lemon juice
1 teaspoon Worcestershire sauce	1 teaspoon Worcestershire sauce
8 oz./225 g. Cheddar cheese, finely grated	2 cups finely grated Cheddar cheese
2 oz./50 g. peeled shrimps	⅓ cup shelled shrimp
4 oz./100 g. cooked green peas	¾ cup cooked green peas

Lightly sauté onion in melted butter until tender. Add the flour and, stirring, cook gently for about a minute. Add the milk gradually, stir constantly until the sauce has thickened. Whisk in the stock, and season. Bring to the boil, stir in cheese, shrimps and peas. Remove from heat and continue stirring until cheese has dissolved. Serve at once.

Tomato Cheese Toasties

Cooking time 7 minutes
Serves 4

Imperial/Metric	American
good ½ oz./20 g. butter	scant 2 tablespoons butter
good ½ oz./20 g. flour	3 tablespoons flour
½ pint/3 dl. milk	1¼ cups milk
½ teaspoon prepared mustard	½ teaspoon prepared mustard
cayenne pepper	cayenne
8 oz./225 g. Cheddar cheese, grated	2 cups grated Cheddar cheese
4 slices buttered toast	4 slices buttered toast
4 tomatoes, skinned and sliced	4 tomatoes, skinned and sliced
2 rashers bacon, cut across in half	2 bacon slices, cut across in half

Melt the butter, add the flour and cook for a minute. Remove from heat. Add the milk gradually, stirring, bring to the boil and cook for a minute. Remove from heat, add the seasonings and grated cheese and stir until the cheese has melted. Prepare the toast and grill the bacon. Arrange the tomato slices on the toast and put under the grill to heat through. Pour the hot cheese sauce over and garnish with crisp pieces of bacon.

Cheese Baked Potatoes

Cooking time 1¼–1½ hours
Oven temperature
350°F., 180°C., Gas Mark 4
Serves 4

Imperial/Metric	American
4 medium potatoes	4 medium potatoes
2 tablespoons milk	2–3 tablespoons milk
good pinch of salt and cayenne pepper	good pinch of salt and cayenne
4 oz./100 g. Cheddar cheese, grated	1 cup grated Cheddar cheese
1 tablespoon chopped parsley	1 tablespoon chopped parsley

Wash and scrub the potatoes, and prick with a fork. Bake in a moderate oven until they feel soft when pinched, about 1¼–1½ hours. Cut each potato in half and scoop out the cooked part, mash with a fork. Beat in the milk, seasonings and lastly the grated cheese and chopped parsley. Return the mixture to the potato-skin 'shells' and reheat in the oven for a few minutes. Serve on their own, or with cold meat.

Raised pork and apple pie, page 37

Potato Cheese Pie

Cooking time 1 hour
Oven temperature
350°F., 180°C., Gas Mark 4
Serves 4

Imperial/Metric	American
8 oz./225 g. Cheddar cheese, grated	2 cups grated Cheddar cheese
2 lb./1 kg. raw potatoes, thinly sliced	2 lb. raw potatoes, thinly sliced
1 oz./25 g. butter	2 tablespoons butter
½ pint/3 dl. milk	1¼ cups milk
salt and pepper	salt and pepper
2 eggs	2 eggs
breadcrumbs	bread crumbs
¼ teaspoon grated nutmeg	¼ teaspoon grated nutmeg

Put alternate layers of grated cheese and thinly sliced
potatoes into a buttered fireproof dish, ending with
grated cheese. Melt the butter in the milk, season well
and pour on to the well beaten eggs. Pour this mixture
over the potato and cheese, add a sprinkling of
breadcrumbs and a little nutmeg, if liked. Bake in a
moderate oven for about 1 hour, until the potatoes are
cooked and the top nicely brown. Serve hot.

Shown in colour on page 27

Pan Haggerty

Cooking time 30 minutes
Serves 4

Imperial/Metric	American
1 lb./450 g. peeled potatoes	1 lb. pared potatoes
8 oz./225 g. onions	½ lb. onions
1 oz./25 g. butter	2 tablespoons butter
6 oz./175 g. Cheddar cheese, grated	1½ cups grated Cheddar cheese
salt and pepper	salt and pepper

Slice the potatoes very thinly and dry off in a cloth.
Slice onions thinly. Melt the butter in a frying pan and
put in a layer of potato, the onions, then grated cheese,
and finish with another layer of potato. Season
between each layer. Fry gently for about 25 minutes,
or until cooked, then place under grill for a further
5 minutes to brown.

Asparagus with Cheese Sauce

Cooking time about 7 minutes
Serves 4

Imperial/Metric	American
1 lb./450 g. cooked green asparagus tips	1 lb. cooked green asparagus tips
for sauce	**for sauce**
2 tablespoons water	3 tablespoons water
2 teaspoons wine vinegar	2 teaspoons wine vinegar
2 egg yolks	2 egg yolks
2 oz./50 g. butter	¼ cup butter
salt and cayenne pepper	salt and cayenne
2 teaspoons lemon juice	2 teaspoons lemon juice
3 oz./75 g. Cheddar cheese, grated	¾ cup grated Cheddar cheese
for garnish	**for garnish**
paprika pepper	paprika

Arrange the drained asparagus on a serving dish.
Cover and keep warm. Put water, wine vinegar and
egg yolks in a bowl over a pan of hot water and whisk
well until thickened. Whisk in the butter in small
pieces, then add seasonings, lemon juice and cheese,
and mix thoroughly. Spoon sauce over asparagus, and
garnish with paprika pepper.

Cheese Medley

Cooking time 1 hour 10 minutes
Oven temperature
375°F., 190°C., Gas Mark 5
Serves 4

Imperial/Metric	American
1½ oz./40 g. butter	3 tablespoons butter
3 medium onions, sliced	3 medium onions, sliced
1 medium swede, sliced	1 medium swede, sliced
1 lb./450 g. carrots, sliced	1 lb. carrots, sliced
salt and pepper	salt and pepper
8 oz./225 g. back bacon rashers, cut into quarters	½ lb. Canadian bacon slices, cut into quarters
for sauce	**for sauce**
1 oz./25 g. butter	2 tablespoons butter
1 oz./25 g. plain flour	¼ cup all-purpose flour
½ pint/3 dl. milk	1¼ cups milk
4 oz./100 g. Cheddar cheese, grated	1 cup grated Cheddar cheese
salt and pepper	salt and pepper
pinch of ground nutmeg	pinch of grated nutmeg
for topping	**for topping**
2 oz./50 g. Cheddar cheese, grated	½ cup grated Cheddar cheese
1 oz./25 g. browned crumbs	¼ cup browned bread crumbs

Melt the butter in a large frying pan, and gently fry onions, swede and carrots for about 20 minutes, turning frequently. Season. Turn half the vegetable mixture into a large ovenproof dish and cover with pieces of bacon. Arrange remaining vegetable mixture over bacon.

For sauce

Melt butter in a small pan, add flour and cook for a minute. Remove from heat, and stir in milk gradually. Return to heat and bring to the boil, stirring. Cook for a minute, remove from heat, and stir in cheese, seasonings and nutmeg. Stir until cheese has melted, and pour sauce over vegetables in dish. Top with cheese and crumbs mixed together, and bake in a moderately hot oven for about 45 minutes, until top is browned and vegetables completely tender.

Cauliflower Cheese

Cooking time about 30 minutes
Serves 4

Imperial/Metric	American
1 cauliflower	1 cauliflower
for cheese sauce	**for cheese sauce**
1 oz./25 g. butter	2 tablespoons butter
1 oz./25 g. plain flour	¼ cup all-purpose flour
½ pint/3 dl. milk (or milk and cauliflower water)	1¼ cups milk (or milk and cauliflower water)
3 oz./75 g. Cheddar cheese, grated	¾ cup grated Cheddar cheese
½ level teaspoon salt	½ teaspoon salt
1 level teaspoon made mustard	1 teaspoon prepared mustard
pinch nutmeg	pinch of nutmeg
for topping	**for topping**
1 oz./25 g. extra grated Cheddar cheese	¼ cup extra grated Cheddar cheese
1 tablespoon browned crumbs	1 tablespoon browned crumbs

Soak the cauliflower in cold water for about 15 minutes, then break into flowerets. Cook in a little boiling water in a covered pan until tender, and arrange neatly in buttered scallop shells or a fireproof dish.

For cheese sauce

Melt the butter, add the flour and cook for 1 minute. Remove from heat and add the milk gradually. Bring to the boil, stirring well. Cook for a minute, remove from the heat, add the seasonings and grated Cheddar cheese, and stir until the cheese has melted. Coat the cauliflower with the cheese sauce. Sprinkle over the mixed grated cheese and browned crumbs. Brown under a hot grill.

Farmhouse Cheese Cake

Cooking time about 35 minutes
Oven temperature
375°F., 190°C., Gas Mark 5
Serves 4–6

Imperial/Metric	American
6 oz./175 g. short crust pastry (see page 44)	6 oz. basic pie dough (see page 44)
for filling	**for filling**
2 oz./50 g. butter	¼ cup butter
1 oz./25 g. castor sugar	2 tablespoons granulated sugar
1 beaten egg	1 beaten egg
6 oz./175 g. Cheddar cheese, finely grated	1½ cups finely grated Cheddar cheese
3 tablespoons milk	4 tablespoons milk
1½ oz./40 g. seedless raisins	¼ cup seedless raisins
½ oz./15 g. chopped mixed peel	good 1 tablespoon chopped mixed candied peel
grated rind of ½ lemon	grated rind of ½ lemon

Roll the pastry out thinly on a lightly floured board. Use to line a deep pie plate, trim and decorate edges.

For filling

Cream the butter and sugar until light and fluffy, then add egg, cheese, milk, raisins, peel and lemon rind. Mix well and turn into pie plate. Decorate top of cheese cake with pastry trimmings. Bake in a moderately hot oven for about 35 minutes. Cool and serve.

Pears Tansy

Serves 4–6

Imperial/Metric	American
¼ pint/1½ dl. soured cream	⅔ cup sour cream
8 oz./225 g. Cheddar cheese, grated	2 cups grated Cheddar cheese
4 level tablespoons blackcurrant jam	5 tablespoons black currant jam
½ oz./15 g. walnuts, chopped	scant ¼ cup chopped walnuts
3 large ripe pears	3 large ripe pears
lemon juice	lemon juice
for decoration	**for decoration**
walnut halves	walnut halves

Put the soured cream, cheese, blackcurrant jam and chopped walnuts into a basin and mix well. Peel, halve and core pears, brush with lemon juice, and arrange on a serving dish. Spoon filling on to centres of pears, top each with a halved walnut, and serve as dessert.

Salad Dishes

New Potato Salad

Cooking time 15–20 minutes
Serves 4

Imperial/Metric	American
1 lb./450 g. new potatoes	1 lb. new potatoes
¼ pint/1½ dl. double cream	⅔ cup heavy cream
1 tablespoon lemon juice	good 1 tablespoon lemon juice
salt and paprika pepper	salt and paprika
1 tablespoon chopped chives	1 tablespoon chopped chives

Scrub or scrape the potatoes and cook in boiling salted water until just tender, 15–20 minutes. Drain well and dice. Whip the cream, add lemon juice, potatoes, seasoning and chopped chives. Leave in refrigerator or cool place until ready to serve.

Hot Potato Salad

Cooking time about 25 minutes
Serves 4

Imperial/Metric	American
1 lb./450 g. potatoes	1 lb. potatoes
1 small onion, finely chopped	1 small onion, finely chopped
3 tablespoons salad oil	4 tablespoons salad oil
1 tablespoon malt vinegar	good 1 tablespoon malt vinegar
salt and pepper	salt and pepper

Boil the potatoes gently in their skins until just cooked. Remove skins and cut potatoes into slices. Fry onion gently in oil for a few minutes until just soft, add vinegar and seasoning, pour over the potatoes.

Ham Salad

Serves 4

Imperial/Metric	American
1 lb./450 g. potatoes, cooked and diced	4 cups diced boiled potatoes
8 oz./225 g. beetroot, cooked and diced	½ lb. beets, boiled and diced
3–4 tablespoons salad cream	4 tablespoons boiled salad dressing
1 lettuce	1 lettuce
2 dessert apples	2 dessert apples
juice of ½ lemon	juice of ½ lemon
8 oz./225 g. cooked ham	½ lb. cooked ham
2 oz./50 g. walnuts, chopped	½ cup chopped walnuts
2 teaspoons chopped parsley	2 teaspoons chopped parsley

Mix the potato and beetroot with enough salad cream to moisten. Wash and shred the lettuce. Peel, core and slice apples thinly then sprinkle with lemon juice to preserve colour. Cut ham into thin strips. Combine apples, walnuts and ham, and place in two bands on a flat dish. Fill the middle with lettuce, and arrange bands of potato and beetroot salad sprinkled with chopped parsley on the outside.

Country Salad

Serves 4

Imperial/Metric	American
1 bunch radishes	1 bunch radishes
1 bunch spring onions	1 bunch scallions
1 head endive	1 head chicory
1 bunch watercress	1 bunch water cress
4 oz./100 g. Leicester cheese	1 cup diced Leicester cheese and
4 oz./100 g. Wensleydale cheese	1 cup diced Wensleydale cheese or use two mild hard cheeses as available
2 hard-boiled eggs	2 hard-cooked eggs
paprika pepper	paprika

Wash all salad foods and drain well. Cut the radishes and spring onions into slices. Place endive and watercress in salad bowl and toss with radishes and onions. Cut cheese into small neat cubes; pile into centre of dish. Garnish with sliced hard-boiled eggs sprinkled with a little paprika pepper.

January Salad

Cooking time 5 minutes
Serves 4

Imperial/Metric	American
8 oz./225 g. beetroot, cooked	½ lb. beets, boiled
8 oz/225 g. Bramley's Seedling apples	½ lb. Bramley's Seedling or other cooking apples
4 oz./100 g. Cheddar cheese	1 cup grated Cheddar cheese
a little lemon juice	a little lemon juice
salt and pepper	salt and pepper
watercress	water cress
8 rashers streaky bacon	8 bacon slices

Coarsely grate the peeled beetroot, apples and cheese. Mix together with lemon juice and seasoning. Serve on a bed of watercress on a flat dish. Cut off the bacon rinds, roll each rasher into a curl, grill quickly and lay on top of the salad.

Somerset bramble and apple pie, page 10
Somerset apples, page 10

Summer Beef Salad

Serves 4

Imperial/Metric	American
1 lb./450 g. cold rare roast beef	1 lb. cold rare-roasted beef
2 eating apples, peeled, cored and diced	2 eating apples, pared, cored and diced
2 celery sticks, diced	2 celery stalks, diced
4 shallots, finely chopped	4 shallots, finely chopped
1 small garlic clove, crushed	1 small garlic clove, crushed
4 tablespoons finely chopped parsley	5 tablespoons finely chopped parsley
lettuce	lettuce
endive	chicory
for dressing	**for dressing**
6 tablespoons salad oil	7 tablespoons salad oil
2–3 tablespoons wine vinegar	3 tablespoons wine vinegar
salt and freshly ground black pepper	salt and freshly milled black pepper

Summer Beef Salad

Trim and dice the beef. Combine beef, apples, celery, shallots with garlic and parsley. Line a salad bowl with leaves of lettuce and endive. Whisk oil with the vinegar and seasoning. Pour dressing over salad just before serving.

Harvest Salad

Serves 4

Imperial/Metric	American
½ pint/3 dl. soured cream	1¼ cups sour cream
few drops Tabasco sauce	few drops Tabasco sauce
pinch of dry mustard	pinch of dry mustard
salt and pepper	salt and pepper
2 tablespoons lemon juice	2 tablespoons lemon juice
3 medium eating apples	3 medium eating apples
1 lb./450 g. fresh blackberries	1 lb. fresh blackberries
1 level tablespoon castor sugar	1 tablespoon granulated sugar
8 oz./225 g. Cheddar cheese, coarsely grated	2 cups coarsely grated Cheddar cheese
for garnish	**for garnish**
paprika pepper	paprika

Mix together soured cream, Tabasco sauce, mustard, seasonings, and half the lemon juice. Peel, core and slice apples, and sprinkle with remaining lemon juice. Mix blackberries with castor sugar.

Arrange half the apple in base of a deep serving dish, cover with half the blackberries, then half the cheese and half the soured cream mixture. Continue layers with remaining ingredients finishing with soured cream mixture on top. Garnish with paprika pepper. Serve with cooked cold ham or pork.

Mushroom Cream Salad

Serves 4

Imperial/Metric	American
4 oz./100 g. mushrooms	1 cup chopped mushrooms
3 hard-boiled eggs	3 hard-cooked eggs
¼ peeled cucumber	¼ peeled cucumber
½ teaspoon dry mustard	½ teaspoon dry mustard
½ teaspoon grated horseradish	½ teaspoon grated horseradish
¼ pint/1½ dl. thick sour cream	⅔ cup heavy sour cream
salt and pepper	salt and pepper
lettuce	lettuce
4 tomatoes, sliced	4 tomatoes, sliced

Finely chop the mushrooms, eggs and cucumber. Blend mustard and horseradish with the cream, adding salt and pepper. Stir in the chopped ingredients. Arrange lettuce leaves on a dish, spoon in cream mixture and circle with tomato slices.

Tomato Delights

Serves 4

Imperial/Metric	American
8 large firm tomatoes	8 large firm tomatoes
8 oz./225 g. boiled potatoes	2 cups diced boiled potatoes
2 tablespoons salad cream	3 tablespoons boiled salad dressing
1 tablespoon chopped parsley	1 tablespoon chopped parsley
½ pint/3 dl. prawns or shrimps	1¼ cups prawns or shrimp
parsley to garnish	parsley to garnish
small lettuce	small lettuce

Wipe the tomatoes with a clean cloth. Stand stalk-end down and cut off each top with a sharp knife. Use handle of a teaspoon to scoop out pulp into a dish. Mix drained pulp with finely diced potatoes, salad cream and chopped parsley.

Peel prawns or shrimps, reserving head for decoration. Leave eight prawns or shrimps whole. Chop remainder finely; add to potato mixture. Pile into tomato cases and top each with whole prawn or shrimp and a small sprig of parsley. Arrange on a bed of lettuce and garnish with a few prawn heads.

Fish Ways

Great Britain has a stirring history of mastery over the sea, that most turbulent of elements, as sailors and fishermen. No other country in Europe has access to such nourishing and delicious sea foods. Our rivers, too, provide a rich fish harvest. It is almost a traditional duty to cook fish well and creatively.

Today we have the advantage of our forefathers: until quite recently only coastal dwellers could enjoy good, really fresh fish. Nowadays most of us can buy, cook and enjoy the best of fish. And what wonderful variety: from familiar herring and cod to special treats like lobster and salmon.

Fish is a very nutritious food with a high protein content. Here are some tips on care and cooking.

If possible eat fish on day of purchase. If it has to be stored overnight, wash and put in clean covered container in refrigerator or cold larder.

To scale fish hold by tail and scrape very firmly with the back of knife towards head.

To skin fillets take fillet in left hand, skin side down, holding it by tip. Make a firm cut with sharp knife at tip, then lift flesh away from skin, continue until all flesh is free. Dip knife edge in salt for a better cutting edge.

Never over-cook fish as the flavour is easily lost. Fish is cooked when the flesh has just shrunk away from the bone or skin, or in the case of fillets the flakes should separate easily.

To poach fish means to simmer gently in salted water or fish stock. Suitable for large fish, like salmon and haddock, having a strong flavour.

Grilling is an excellent method for fillets, cutlets and small whole fish. The prepared fish should always be brushed with a little oil or melted fat, and may be sprinkled with coarse oatmeal or dried breadcrumbs. The grill should be pre-heated before the fish is placed under.

Baking is a tasty method for most kinds of fish.

Steamed fish is often recommended for invalids because it is so easy to digest. Season and sprinkle with lemon juice before steaming, drain well and serve with a plain sauce or garnish.

Potato cheese pie, page 20

Ocean Pie

Cooking time 30 minutes
Oven temperature
425°F., 220°C., Gas Mark 7
Serves 4

Imperial/Metric	American
8 oz./225 g. smoked haddock	*½ lb. smoked haddock (finnan haddie)*
2 scallops	*2 scallops*
4 oz./100 g. soft roes	*¼ lb. soft roe (milt)*
salt and pepper	*salt and pepper*
4 oz./100 g. mushrooms	*1 cup mushrooms*
3 oz./75 g. prawns, peeled	*½ cup shrimp or scampi, shelled*
½ pint/3 dl. white sauce (see page 29)	*1¼ cups white sauce (see page 29)*
⅛ pint/¾ dl. thick cream	*⅓ cup whipping cream*
2 lb./900 g. fluffy, creamed potatoes	*2 lb. fluffy, creamed potatoes*

Cut the haddock into 3-inch/7-cm. squares. Clean and chop the scallops and roes, and arrange in a fireproof dish. Season. Place the haddock on top. Slice the mushrooms and add with the prawns to the white sauce. Simmer for 5 minutes, then stir in the cream away from the heat. Pour the sauce over the fish and top with the creamy potatoes. Cook in a hot oven for about 25 minutes.

Finnan Haddock in Mushroom Cream

Cooking time 30 minutes
Oven temperature
375°F., 190°C., Gas Mark 5
Serves 4

Imperial/Metric	American
4 finnan haddock fillets	*4 smoked haddock (finnan haddie) fillets*
8 oz./225 g. mushrooms	*2 cups mushrooms*
freshly ground black pepper	*freshly milled black pepper*
½ pint/3 dl. milk	*1¼ cups milk*
2 oz./50 g. butter	*¼ cup butter*
¼ pint/1½ dl. double cream	*⅔ cup whipping cream*
for garnish	**for garnish**
paprika pepper, lemon wedges	*paprika, lemon wedges*

Place the fillets in an ovenproof dish and slice the mushrooms over the top. Sprinkle generously with freshly ground black pepper, pour over the milk and dot with butter. Cover dish and bake in a moderately hot oven for about 25 minutes. Strain milk from the fish and mix with the cream, replace in the oven for a few minutes to heat through. Serve sprinkled with paprika pepper and garnished with lemon wedges.

Country Fish Pie

Cooking time about 30 minutes
Serves 4

Imperial/Metric	American
1½ lb./675 g. cod fillet	*1½ lb. cod fillet*
approx. 1 pint/6 dl. water to cover	*approx. 2½ cups water to cover*
strip of lemon rind	*strip of lemon rind*
1 bay leaf	*1 bay leaf*
salt and pepper	*salt and pepper*
2 oz./50 g. butter or margarine	*¼ cup butter or margarine*
1½ oz./40 g. plain flour	*⅓ cup all-purpose flour*
½ pint/3 dl. milk	*1¼ cups milk*
2 tablespoons chopped parsley	*good 2 tablespoons chopped parsley*
2 hard-boiled eggs	*2 hard-cooked eggs*
for topping	**for topping**
1 lb./450 g. freshly boiled potatoes	*1 lb. freshly boiled potatoes*
1 oz./25 g. cheese, finely grated	*¼ cup finely grated cheese*
for garnish	**for garnish**
1 tomato, sliced	*1 tomato, sliced*
parsley sprigs	*parsley sprigs*

Wipe the cod and place in a large saucepan with water to cover. Add the lemon rind, bay leaf and salt and pepper. Bring to the boil then simmer gently about 15 minutes. Remove the fish with a draining spoon, discard any skin and bones and flake into small pieces.

Melt the butter or margarine in a saucepan. Sprinkle in the flour and cook for 2 minutes, stirring. Gradually blend in the milk and ¼ pint/1½ dl. strained fish liquor. Bring to the boil then simmer gently 2–3 minutes, stirring throughout to make a smooth sauce. Add the flaked fish, chopped parsley, and roughly chopped hard-boiled eggs. Season to taste if necessary. Pour into a deep pie dish or ovenproof dish. Surround

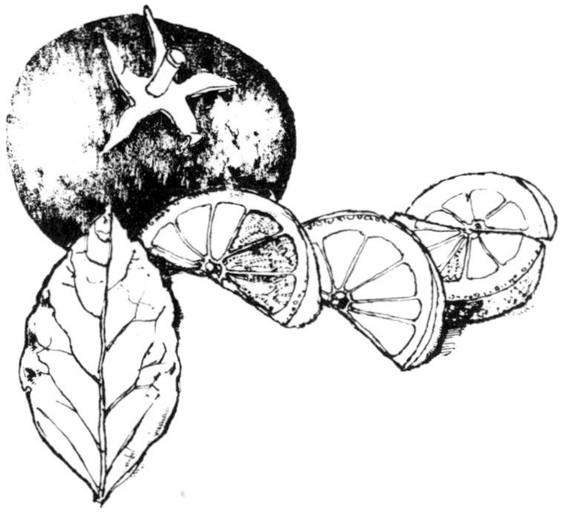

with thinly sliced cooked potatoes and sprinkle with finely grated cheese. Place under a hot grill until golden brown and crisp. Decorate with chopped tomato and sprigs of parsley.

Shown in colour on page 31

Cod in Cider

Cooking time 30 minutes
Oven temperature
375°F., 190°C., Gas Mark 5
Serves 4

Imperial/Metric	American
1 lb./450 g. cod fillet	1 lb. cod fillet
4 oz./100 g. mushrooms	1 cup mushrooms
2 large tomatoes, halved	2 large tomatoes, halved
½ pint/3 dl. cider	1¼ cups cider
salt and pepper	salt and pepper
1 oz./25 g. butter	2 tablespoons butter
1 oz./25 g. plain flour	¼ cup all-purpose flour
2–3 oz./50–75 g. cheese, grated	½–¾ cup grated cheese

Cut the cod into four serving pieces, and arrange in a greased fireproof dish with the mushrooms and tomatoes. Pour the cider slowly over all the ingredients in the dish and then season them with salt and pepper. Bake for about 25 minutes in a moderately hot oven.

Meanwhile, melt the fat, add the flour and cook for a few minutes. Add the liquid from the fish, bring to the boil and cook gently, stirring, for a few minutes. Pour this sauce over the fish, sprinkle with the grated cheese and brown under a hot grill.

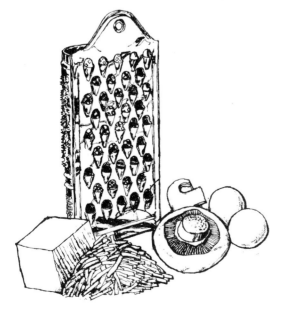

Devilled Halibut

Cooking time 25–35 minutes
Oven temperature
375°F., 190°C., Gas Mark 5
Serves 4

Imperial/Metric	American
4 halibut steaks	4 halibut steaks
3 oz./75 g. butter or margarine	6 tablespoons butter or margarine
2–3 oz./50–75 g. fresh breadcrumbs	1–1½ cups soft fresh bread crumbs
¼ pint/1½ dl. thick white sauce (see below)	⅔ cup thick white sauce (see below)
½ teaspoon anchovy essence	1 teaspoon anchovy paste
2 teaspoons made mustard	2 teaspoons prepared mustard
1 tablespoon chopped piccalilli	1 tablespoon chopped piccalilli
good pinch each : salt, pepper and cayenne	good pinch each : salt, pepper and cayenne

Wipe the halibut steaks and place in base of grill pan. Dot with 2 oz./50 g. of the butter and cook under a medium grill for 10–15 minutes or until just tender. Transfer to an overproof dish, pour over any juices from the pan. Place breadcrumbs on a baking sheet in a moderately hot oven for 5 minutes or until pale golden brown.

Blend thick white sauce, anchovy essence, made mustard, chopped piccalilli and seasonings together. Spread over fish steaks and sprinkle with browned breadcrumbs. Dot with remaining butter, bake in a moderately hot oven for 15–20 minutes. Serve very hot.

White Sauce

Makes ½ pint/3 dl.

Imperial/Metric	American
1 oz./25 g. butter or margarine	2 tablespoons butter or margarine
1 oz./25 g. plain flour	¼ cup all-purpose flour
½ pint/3 dl. milk	1¼ cups milk
salt and pepper	salt and pepper

Melt butter or margarine in a small pan, but do not allow to brown. Remove from the heat, stir in the flour. Stir over gentle heat for about 1 minute until mixture bubbles and looks like honeycomb. Remove the pan from heat and gradually blend in milk, a little at a time, beating well to avoid lumps. Season to taste. Return pan to gentle heat, bring to the boil, simmer gently, stirring all the time for 3 minutes, to form a smooth, glossy sauce, thick enough to coat the back of a spoon.

Buttered Trout

Cooking time about 12 minutes
Serves 4

Imperial/Metric	American
4 medium trout	4 medium trout
1 tablespoon seasoned flour	1 tablespoon seasoned flour
4–6 oz./100–175 g. butter	½–¾ cup butter
2 tablespoons lemon juice	good 2 tablespoons lemon juice
1 tablespoon chopped parsley	1 tablespoon chopped parsley

Clean and gut the trout, wipe fish with a clean damp cloth then toss in seasoned flour to coat. Melt the butter in a frying pan and fry trout gently, turning once during cooking until nicely browned and cooked through, about 10 minutes. Transfer to a serving dish. Stir lemon juice and parsley into remaining butter in pan and heat through; pour over fish.

Grilled Salmon

Cooking time about 12–16 minutes
Serves 4

Imperial/Metric	American
4 salmon steaks (middle cut)	4 salmon steaks (middle cut)
2 oz./50 g. melted butter	¼ cup melted butter
salt and pepper	salt and pepper
parsley butter (see below)	parsley butter (see below)
for garnish	**for garnish**
lemon wedges	lemon wedges

Wipe the fish with a clean damp cloth, then brush over with melted butter. Season to taste with salt and pepper and place the steaks on a well greased grill rack. Grill each side 6–8 minutes, according to thickness of slices or until steaks are cooked through.

Serve each steak topped with parsley butter. Garnish with lemon wedges.

Parsley Butter

Imperial/Metric	American
2 oz./50 g. unsalted butter	¼ cup sweet (unsalted) butter
2 teaspoons chopped parsley	2 teaspoons chopped parsley
few drops of lemon juice	few drops of lemon juice
salt and pepper	salt and pepper

Soften the butter on a plate with a palette knife, then work in the parsley, lemon juice and seasoning to taste. Serve chilled in pats.

Note
Also suitable for serving with mixed grills and steak.

Kipper Cakes

Cooking time about 15 minutes
Serves 4

Imperial/Metric	American
8 oz./225 g. cooked kipper fillets	½ lb. cooked kipper fillets
8 oz./225 g. mashed potato	1 cup mashed potatoes
1 oz./25 g. butter	2 tablespoons butter
1 beaten egg	1 beaten egg
1 teaspoon chopped parsley	1 teaspoon chopped parsley
salt and pepper	salt and pepper
for coating	**for coating**
1 beaten egg	1 beaten egg
2 tablespoons browned breadcrumbs	2 tablespoons browned bread crumbs
for frying	**for frying**
fat	fat

In a large bowl mix together flaked kipper, mashed potato, softened butter, beaten egg and parsley. Season well with a little salt and with pepper. Divide mixture into four and mould into round cakes.

Dip the cakes into egg and then in breadcrumbs. Fry in hot fat on both sides until golden brown. Drain on crumpled kitchen paper and serve at once.

Baked Buttered Bloaters

Cooking time 10 minutes
Oven temperature
350°F., 180°C., Gas Mark 4
Serves 4

Imperial/Metric	American
4 bloaters	4 bloaters (or kippers)
2 oz./50 g. butter	¼ cup butter
2 tablespoons lemon juice	good 2 tablespoons lemon juice
salt and pepper	salt and pepper
4 slices buttered toast	4 slices buttered toast

Cut off heads, tails and fins and bone bloaters. Put in a greased ovenproof dish, dot with butter and season well with lemon juice, salt and pepper. Cover and bake for 10 minutes in a moderate oven. Pile on hot buttered toast.

Country fish pie, page 28
Chicken and ham croquettes, page 41

Herrings in Ale

Cooking time 1–1½ hours
Oven temperature
275°F., 140°C., Gas Mark 1
Serves 4

Imperial/Metric	American
4–6 herrings	4–6 herring
salt and pepper	salt and pepper
about ½ pint/3 dl. ale	about 1¼ cups ale
2 teaspoons mixed pickling spice	2 teaspoons mixed pickling spice
4 bay leaves	4 bay leaves
2 small onions	2 small onions

Clean, split and fillet the herrings. Season well with salt and pepper. Roll them up, skin inwards, beginning at the tail. Place them neatly and fairly close together in an ovenproof dish. Cover with the ale and sprinkle with mixed pickling spice. Garnish with bay leaves and rings of onion. Bake in a cool oven.

Note

If liked, ½ oz./15 g. powdered aspic jelly can be added to the liquid after cooking. Allow herrings to cool in the liquid as it sets.

Herrings with Red Cabbage

Cooking time 2 hours 10 minutes
Oven temperature
350°F., 180°C., Gas Mark 4
Serves 4

Imperial/Metric	American
1 oz./25 g. butter	2 tablespoons butter
2 medium onions, chopped	2 medium onions, chopped
1½ lb./675 g. red cabbage, finely shredded	1½ lb. red cabbage, finely shredded
3 oz./75 g. soft brown sugar	6 tablespoons brown sugar
4 tablespoons wine vinegar	5 tablespoons wine vinegar
salt and pepper	salt and pepper
4 herrings	4 herring
for garnish	**for garnish**
lemon slices	lemon slices

Melt the butter in a pan or in a fireproof casserole. Add the onion and fry for about 5 minutes until soft and golden. Add red cabbage and cook for a further 5 minutes. Stir in sugar and vinegar. Season with salt and pepper. If in a pan, transfer at this stage to an ovenproof casserole. Cover. Bake in a moderate oven for 2 hours, or until tender.

Clean herrings and place them on top of the red cabbage for the last 20 minutes of the cooking time. Garnish with lemon slices.

Herrings with Red Cabbage

Crab Salads

Serves 4

Imperial/Metric	American
8 oz./225 g. cooked crab meat	½ lb. cooked crab meat
2 hard-boiled eggs	2 hard-cooked eggs
¼ cucumber	¼ cucumber
3 tablespoons mayonnaise (see page 17)	4 tablespoons mayonnaise (see page 17)
1 lettuce	1 lettuce
for garnish	**for garnish**
watercress sprigs	water cress sprigs

Flake the crab and mix with chopped eggs and diced cucumber in a bowl. Bind together with the mayonnaise. Place a bed of shredded lettuce on each of four scallop shells. Divide crab mixture between shells and garnish with watercress. Serve with thinly sliced brown bread and butter.

Lobster Mayonnaise

Serves 4

Imperial/Metric	American
2 medium cooked lobsters	2 medium cooked lobsters
¼ pint/1½ dl. mayonnaise (see (see page 17)	⅔ cup mayonnaise (see page 17)
lettuce	lettuce
sliced tomatoes	sliced tomatoes
sliced cucumber	sliced cucumber
watercress	water cress

Split each lobster with a sharp knife down the centre. Open the halves, cut-side uppermost. Remove and discard intestine (long black line running to tail). Discard lady fingers (found where small claws join body). Carefully remove stomach bag, situated near head. Reserve bright pink coral for garnish. Remove the large claws, then crack with a weight. Take out flesh from the claws in one piece if possible and add to other flesh scooped out from body of lobster.

Mix lobster meat with mayonnaise, then pile back into shells and decorate with coral. Serve on a bed of lettuce with tomato and cucumber slices and watercress.

Seafood Platter

Serves 4

Imperial/Metric	American
8 oz./225 g. cooked crab meat	½ lb. cooked crab meat
1 pint/6 dl. peeled prawns	2½ cups shelled scampi or shrimp
6 oz./175 g. button mushrooms, sliced	1½ cups sliced button mushrooms
6 oz./175 g. cold cooked rice	good 1 cup cold cooked rice
½ pint/3 dl. double cream	1¼ cups whipping cream
1 tablespoon mayonnaise (see page 17)	1 tablespoon mayonnaise (see page 17)
1 teaspoon grated onion	1 teaspoon grated onion
a little grated horseradish	a little grated horseradish
salt and pepper	salt and pepper
1 tablespoon chopped chives	1 tablespoon chopped chives

Mix the flaked crab with prawns, mushrooms and rice in a bowl. Whip the cream, add mayonnaise, onion and horseradish to taste. Add cream sauce to fish mixture and blend well together. Season to taste. Turn into serving dish and sprinkle with chopped chives.

Meat and Poultry Dinners

It has been said that traditional British cooking has remained simple because meat and poultry, though not always cheap, have usually been plentiful. A roast sirloin or a fat capon needs no artifice – they were, and still are, great meals in their own right.

The country housewife has always excelled at cooking the prime cuts of meat, but her proper sense of thrift has helped her to devise tasty stews, meat puddings and pies. These recipes are of particular interest now that meat is a major budgeting item, and I've included a selection in the recipes that follow. Here are some tips on the care and cooking of meat to help you make the most of this valuable food.

Uncooked meat stored in the larder should be wrapped in muslin and hung from a meat hook, or put on a plate and covered in muslin to protect it from flies.

Uncooked meat stored in the refrigerator should be put in the chiller tray, immediately under the freezer, or on a plate with kitchen foil lying loosely on top. Never put it in a sealed container.

Keep cooked meat which is to be eaten cold in the same way as raw meat in the larder. In the refrigerator, wrap in kitchen foil; remove 30 minutes before serving.

Raw minced meat should be used up the day it is minced.

Offal should not be hung, but eaten as soon as possible after buying.

Frozen and chilled meat de-frost thoroughly before cooking.

Coarse and cheaper cuts of meat are equal in food value to prime cuts, but need longer, slower cooking to make them really tender.

Use the residue in the tin or pan when roasting or frying meat as a basis for gravy – these juices are good for you.

If the meat is boned, use the bones to make stock as a basis for soups.

All offal, especially liver, is very nutritious. Try to include it regularly in your diet.

Roasting times don't over-cook and dry up meat when roasting. Weigh your joint and calculate cooking time before putting it in the oven. Good method of roasting is to put joint in pre-heated hot oven (425°F., 220°C., Gas Mark 7) for first 15 minutes, then reduce heat to moderate (350°F., 180°C., Gas Mark 4) for rest of cooking time. As a general rule allow: beef (medium done), mutton and lamb – 20 minutes per lb./450 g. and 20 minutes over; pork – 30 minutes per lb./450 g. and 30 minutes over; veal – 25 minutes per lb./450 g. and 25 minutes over.

When frying place meat in hot shallow fat; this seals in the juices.

Don't use too much liquid in stews and casseroles.

Pre-heat grill before grilling meat, to seal in juices.

Poultry, once a luxury, is now within the reach of the average purse. If you are using the frozen variety, do give it time to thaw out at room temperature before cooking.

Meat Dishes

Roast Beef and Yorkshire Pudding

Cooking time approx. 1¼ hours
Oven temperature
400°F., 200°C., Gas Mark 6
then 425°F., 220°C., Gas Mark 7
Serves 4

Imperial/Metric	American
about 3 lb./1⅓ kg. boned and rolled sirloin of beef	about 3 lb. sirloin of beef, boned and rolled
3 oz./75 g. dripping or lard	6 tablespoons drippings or lard
for Yorkshire pudding	**for Yorkshire pudding**
4 oz./110 g. self-raising or plain flour	1 cup all-purpose flour or all-purpose flour sifted with 1 teaspoon double-acting baking powder
large pinch of salt	large pinch of salt
1 egg	1 egg
½ pint/3 dl. milk	1¼ cups milk

Place weighed joint in a roasting pan and add dripping. Place in a hot oven and roast, allowing 25 minutes per lb./450 g.

Sift flour and salt into bowl. Add egg, then gradually add half the milk, stirring the flour from sides of the bowl using a wooden spoon. Beat well until the mixture is smooth. Gently stir in the rest of the milk. 40 minutes before joint is done increase oven heat to 425°F., 220°C., Gas Mark 7. Remove joint from roasting pan and pour off excess fat. Put a trivet in the centre of the pan and quickly pour in the batter. Place joint on trivet and return to oven as near the top as possible.

Serve as soon as Yorkshire pudding is well risen, crisp and golden brown.

Braised Beef in Cider

Cooking time 1¾–2¼ hours
Oven temperature
375°F., 190°C., Gas Mark 5
Serves 4

Imperial/Metric	American
1 lb./450 g. topside of beef, cut into thin slices	1 lb. beef, rolled rump roast or tip steak, cut into thin slices
seasoned flour	seasoned flour
1½ oz./40 g. dripping	3 tablespoons drippings
8 oz./225 g. onions, sliced	½ lb. onions, sliced
1 bay leaf	1 bay leaf
1 sprig thyme	1 sprig thyme
salt and pepper	salt and pepper
½ pint/3 dl. dry cider	1¼ cups dry cider

Beat slices of meat with a rolling pin until they are very thin, and coat with seasoned flour. Melt the dripping in a frying pan and fry meat for few minutes until browned on both sides. Place in casserole.

Gently fry the onions until soft and add to casserole with herbs and seasoning. Pour over the cider. Cover with lid and cook in a moderately hot oven for 1½–2 hours or until meat is tender; add more cider, if necessary, during cooking.

Casserole of Beef

Cooking time 3–3¼ hours
Oven temperature
325°F., 170°C., Gas Mark 3
Serves 4

Imperial/Metric	American
1½ oz./40 g. cooking fat	3 tablespoons shortening
2 large onions, peeled and sliced	2 large onions, peeled and sliced
1½ lb./675 g. stewing steak	1½ lb. stewing beef
1½ oz./40 g. plain flour	6 tablespoons all-purpose flour
1 level teaspoon curry powder	1 teaspoon curry powder
1 pint/6 dl. beef stock	2½ cups beef stock
2 tablespoons tomato purée	3 tablespoons tomato paste
1 lb./450 g. carrots, peeled and sliced	1 lb. carrots, peeled and sliced
salt and pepper	salt and pepper

Melt the fat in a pan and fry onions until tender, about 5 minutes. Trim and cut the meat into cubes, add to the pan and fry quickly until brown all over. Mix in the flour and curry powder, then blend in the stock, tomato purée, carrots and seasoning to taste.

Bring to the boil, transfer to a casserole, cover and place in a very moderate oven for 2¾–3¼ hours. Serve with boiled potatoes.

Steak and Kidney Pie

Cooking time 2½ hours
Oven temperature
400°F., 200°C., Gas Mark 6
Serves 4

Imperial/Metric	American
8 oz./225 g. short crust or flaky pastry (see page 44)	½ lb. basic or rich flaky pie dough (see page 44)
for filling	**for filling**
1 lb./450 g. stewing steak	1 lb. stewing beef
8 oz./225 g. sheep's kidneys	½ lb. lamb kidneys
1 oz./25 g. dripping	2 tablespoons drippings
1 small onion, chopped	1 small onion, chopped
1 tablespoon plain flour	1 tablespoon all-purpose flour
½ pint/3 dl. stock	1¼ cups stock
salt and pepper	salt and pepper
for glaze	**for glaze**
beaten egg	beaten egg

Trim and cut the steak into cubes. Skin, core and chop kidneys. Melt dripping in a pan, add onion, steak and kidneys and toss in hot fat until lightly browned. Stir in the flour, mix well, then add the stock. Season to taste, bring to the boil, reduce heat and simmer about 1¾ hours or until tender. Place in a 1½-pint/9-dl. pie dish, allow to cool.

Damp edges of pie dish and cover with rolled out pastry. Rough up edges and flute. Make pastry leaves with trimmings and damp before putting on pastry. Brush top of pie with beaten egg.

Bake in hot oven for about 45 minutes or until golden.

Steak, Kidney and Mushroom Pudding

Cooking time 4 hours
Serves 4

Imperial/Metric	American
8 oz./225 g. suet crust pastry (see page 44)	½ lb. suet crust dough (see page 44)
for filling	**for filling**
1 lb./450 g. lean stewing steak	1 lb. lean stewing beef
4 oz./100 g. ox kidney	¼ lb. beef kidney
4 oz./100 g. mushrooms ·	1 cup mushrooms
1 rounded tablespoon plain flour	1–2 tablespoons all-purpose flour
½ level teaspoon salt	½ teaspoon salt
¼ level teaspoon ground pepper	¼ teaspoon milled pepper
approx. 6 tablespoons stock or water	approx. 7 tablespoons (scant ½ cup) stock or water

Trim and cut the meat into small neat pieces. Skin, core and roughly chop kidney. Wipe and slice the mushrooms. Toss the meats and mushrooms in flour, salt and pepper. Line a greased pudding basin with most of rolled out pastry, retaining just enough for the cover.

Place prepared meats and mushrooms in basin, then pour in stock or water nearly to cover. Damp edges of pastry. Roll out rest of pastry for lid, place in position and press edges firmly together to seal. Use sharp knife to trim edges neatly. Cover top closely with aluminium foil.

Place in top of steamer and steam steadily for about 4 hours, refilling bottom pan with boiling water as necessary. Remove foil from pudding. Arrange a clean napkin round the basin for holding and to serve.

Boiled Beef and Dumplings

Cooking time about 2½ hours
Serves 4

Imperial/Metric	American
2 lb./900 g. salt silverside or topside	2 lb. brisket of beef, salted (corned)
cold water to cover	cold water to cover
a bouquet garni (parsley, thyme, bay leaf, tied together)	a bouquet garni (parsley, thyme, bay leaf, tied together)
4 onions, peeled and stuck with cloves	4 onions, peeled and stuck with cloves
1 lb./450 g. carrots, peeled and quartered	1 lb. carrots, peeled and quartered
for dumplings	**for dumplings**
4 oz./110 g. self-raising flour	1 cup all-purpose flour sifted with 1 teaspoon double-acting baking powder
1 level teaspoon salt	1 teaspoon salt
2 oz./50 g. shredded suet	⅓ cup finely chopped beef suet
cold water to mix	cold water to mix

Put the meat into a pan with sufficient cold water to cover and bring slowly to boiling point, and skim. Reduce heat to simmering point. Add the bouquet garni and the onions. Allow to simmer for about 1¼ hours, then remove bouquet garni. Add carrots and continue to simmer for a further 45 minutes, or until vegetables are just tender.

Meanwhile, sift flour with salt and add suet. Mix lightly with cold water to make a fairly soft dough. Divide into about eight pieces and with floured hands, form into balls. Add to meat and vegetables when vegetables are tender, and continue to simmer for another 15–20 minutes.

Serve the meat on a hot dish with the vegetables and dumplings arranged round, a little of the liquor poured on to the dish, and more handed separately in a sauce boat.

Steak in Beer and Mushroom Sauce

Cooking time 30 minutes
Serves 4

Imperial/Metric	American
1½ lb./675 g. rump steak	1½ lb. beef round steak
1 clove garlic	1 clove garlic
4 tablespoons vegetable oil	5 tablespoons vegetable oil
for sauce	**for sauce**
2 oz./50 g. butter	¼ cup butter
8 oz./225 g. mushrooms, sliced	2 cups sliced mushrooms
2 rounded teaspoons cornflour	1 tablespoon cornstarch
½ pint/3 dl. beer	1¼ cups beer
salt and pepper	salt and pepper
1 teaspoon tomato purée	1 teaspoon tomato paste
1 teaspoon Worcestershire sauce	1 teaspoon Worcestershire sauce

Buy the steak cut in one thick slice; cut into good sized cubes. Crush the garlic and simmer this gently in oil in a frying pan. Add the steak and cook gently until sealed and tender, 20 minutes.

Meanwhile, in a saucepan heat the butter and lightly fry mushrooms for about 4 minutes. Blend cornflour with a little of the beer and add to mushrooms, cook for a minute or two, stirring, then add rest of beer. Season and bring to the boil. Add tomato purée and Worcestershire sauce, cook for a minute or two, stirring. Turn steak on to a hot serving plate and pour over the mushroom and beer sauce.

Pork 'n' Parsnips

Cooking time 1½ hours
Oven temperature
400°F., 200°C., Gas Mark 6
Serves 4

Imperial/Metric	American
1 lb./450 g. potatoes	1 lb. potatoes
1 lb./450 g. parsnips	1 lb. parsnips
1½ lb./675 g. belly pork, with skin scored	1½-lb. piece pork, fresh picnic shoulder
salt and pepper	salt and pepper
1 tablespoon redcurrant jelly	good 1 tablespoon red currant jelly

Peel and halve the potatoes and parsnips. Boil in salted water for 2 minutes. Strain and reserve the liquid. Rub the skin of the pork with salt and pepper. Put in a roasting pan with the potatoes and parsnips round it. Add one teacup of the liquid.

Dissolve the redcurrant jelly in another two tablespoons of the liquid and pour over the pork. Cook in hot oven for about 1½ hours.

Raised Pork and Apple Pie

Cooking time 2–2½ hours
Oven temperature
350°F., 180°C., Gas Mark 4
Serves 4–6

Imperial/Metric	American
12 oz./350 g. hot water crust pastry (see below)	¾ lb. hot water crust (see below)
for filling	**for filling**
2 lb./1 kg. pork fillet, diced	2 lb. pork tenderloin, diced
1 apple, peeled, cored and shredded	1 apple, pared, cored and shredded
salt and pepper	salt and pepper
7 tablespoons stock or water	½ cup stock or water
1 beaten egg	1 beaten egg
1 level teaspoon powdered gelatine	1 teaspoon gelatin
½ level teaspoon meat extract	½ teaspoon meat flavoring extract

Line a greased and floured raised pie pan with two-thirds of rolled out pastry. Arrange layers of pork and apple in pan, seasoning each layer with salt and pepper.

Pour in 3 tablespoons stock or water. Damp pastry edges and cover with remaining rolled out pastry, decorate with leaves made from pastry trimmings. Make an air vent in centre, and brush with beaten egg. Bake in centre of a moderate oven for 2–2½ hours. After 1¾ hours, if pastry is firm, remove pan and brush sides with beaten egg.

Leave the cooked pie to cool. Melt gelatine in remaining stock or water, stir in meat extract and allow to cool and partially set. Pour setting gelatine mixture into pie through hole in centre, and leave to set before serving.

Shown in colour on page 19

Hot Water Crust Pastry for Raised Pies

Makes 12 oz./350 g. hot water crust pastry
(¾ lb. hot water pie crust)

Imperial/Metric	American
12 oz./350 g. plain flour	3 cups all-purpose flour
pinch of salt	pinch of salt
4 oz./110 g. lard	½ cup lard
¼ pint/1½ dl. water	⅔ cup water

Sieve the flour and salt into a basin. Melt the fat in warm water and add to flour. Mix with a knife and knead gently with the fingers. Use while still warm.

Poacher's Roll

Poacher's Roll

Cooking time 45 minutes
Oven temperature
375°F., 190°C., Gas Mark 5
Serves 4

Imperial/Metric	American
12 oz./350 g. short crust pastry (see page 44)	¾ lb. basic pie dough (see page 44)
for filling	**for filling**
1 lb./450 g. pork sausage meat	1 lb. pork sausage meat
1 cooking apple, peeled, cored and grated	1 cooking apple, pared, cored and grated
1 small can sweetcorn kernels	1 small can kernel corn
1 teaspoon chopped fresh or dried tarragon	1 teaspoon chopped fresh or dried tarragon
salt and pepper	salt and pepper
for glaze	**for glaze**
beaten egg	beaten egg

Roll out pastry on lightly floured board into an oblong approximately 10 inches by 11 inches (25 cm. by 28 cm.). Mix the filling together and spread over pastry to within an inch of the edge. Brush round edge with beaten egg and roll up pastry as for a sausage roll, place on baking sheet. Brush roll with beaten egg and decorate with pastry circles cut from trimmings, brush these with beaten egg.

Bake in a moderately hot oven for about 45 minutes or until golden. Serve hot or cold, cut into slices.

Devilled Pork Chops

Cooking time about 30 minutes
Serves 4

Imperial/Metric	American
4 lean pork chops	4 lean pork chops
1 tablespoon bacon fat or dripping	1 tablespoon bacon fat or drippings
3 oz./75 g. butter or margarine	6 tablespoons butter or margarine
2 teaspoons dry mustard	2 teaspoons dry mustard
2 teaspoons curry powder or paste	2 teaspoons curry powder or paste
½ teaspoon ground ginger	½ teaspoon ground ginger
½ teaspoon salt	½ teaspoon salt
1 tablespoon Worcestershire sauce	1 tablespoon Worcestershire sauce
8 oz./225 g. fresh white breadcrumbs	4 cups fresh soft white bread crumbs

Trim the chops and fry in fat for 15–20 minutes, depending on thickness, until cooked. Meanwhile, cream butter or margarine with mustard, curry powder or paste, ginger, salt and sauce. When chops are cooked, allow to get cool, then smear the mixture well over the chops. Sprinkle with breadcrumbs and put under hot grill for a few minutes until breadcrumbs are golden brown.

Roast Stuffed Loin of Lamb

Cooking time approx. 1½ hours
Oven temperature
425°F., 220°C., Gas Mark 7 for 15 minutes,
350°F., 180°C., Gas Mark 4 for 1¼ hours
Serves 4–6

Imperial/Metric	American
about 3 lb./1⅓ kg. boned loin of lamb	about 3 lb. lamb, rolled double loin
a little dripping	little drippings
for stuffing	**for stuffing**
3 oz./75 g. fresh white breadcrumbs	1½ cups soft fresh white bread crumbs
1½ oz./40 g. shredded suet	¼ cup finely chopped beef suet
½ teaspoon mixed herbs	½ teaspoon mixed herbs
grated rind of ½ lemon	grated rind of ½ lemon
salt and pepper	salt and pepper
beaten egg	beaten egg

Mix the breadcrumbs with suet, herbs, lemon rind and seasoning. Add sufficient beaten egg to mix to a stiff consistency. Put stuffing neatly where the bone was removed from joint. Roll up and tie in several places with fine string. Weigh joint and calculate cooking time, allowing 20 minutes to the lb./450 g., and 20 minutes over.

Put the stuffed joint in a roasting pan, dot with dripping and roast in a hot oven for the first 15 minutes, reduce heat to moderate for rest of cooking time, baste now and then.

Lamb Casserole with Crusty Topping

Cooking time 2 hours 35 minutes
Oven temperature
325°F., 170°C., Gas Mark 3 for 2 hours,
375°F., 190°C., Gas Mark 5 for 20 minutes
Serves 4–6

Imperial/Metric	American
2 lb./900 g. lamb (meat from shoulder, neck or breast)	2 lb. lamb, arm chops or neck slices
1 oz./25 g. well seasoned flour	¼ cup well seasoned flour
1 oz./25 g. cooking fat, lard or dripping	2 tablespoons shortening, lard or drippings
2 medium onions, peeled and thinly sliced	2 medium onions, peeled and thinly sliced
3 sticks celery, chopped	3 stalks celery, chopped
1 pint/6 dl. water	2½ cups water
2 level tablespoons tomato purée	2 tablespoons tomato paste
¼ teaspoon salt	¼ teaspoon salt
4 well buttered slices of bread	4 well buttered slices of bread

Divide the meat into 1-inch/3-cm. pieces and coat with seasoned flour. Melt the fat in a pan, add vegetables and fry over medium heat until light golden. Move to one side and fry the meat. Transfer to a casserole dish, then pour over the water mixed with the tomato purée and salt. Cover with a lid and cook in a very moderate oven for 2 hours.

Remove casserole from the oven. Cut each slice of bread into four triangles and arrange on top of meat, buttered-side up. Return to a moderately hot oven for 20 minutes until bread is golden brown.

Liver and Bacon Casserole

Cooking time about 1¾ hours
Oven temperature
350°F., 180°C., Gas Mark 4
Serves 4

Imperial/Metric	American
12 oz./350 g. ox liver	¾ lb. beef liver
2 level tablespoons plain flour	3 tablespoons all-purpose flour
salt and pepper	salt and pepper
2 oz./50 g. lard or bacon dripping	¼ cup lard or bacon drippings
8 oz./225 g. onions	½ lb. onions
4 oz./100 g. streaky bacon	¼ lb. bacon slices
8 oz./225 g. carrots	½ lb. carrots
½ pint/3 dl. stock or water	1¼ cups stock or water
1 lb./450 g. potatoes	1 lb. potatoes

Wash, dry and cut the liver into slices. Coat with the flour, seasoned with salt and pepper. Melt the fat in a frying pan and fry the liver and peeled and sliced onions until brown. Transfer the liver and onions to a casserole. Add the trimmed bacon and peeled and sliced carrots. Mix any remaining flour into the fat in the frying pan and then blend in the stock or water and seasoning to taste and bring to the boil, still stirring. Pour into the casserole and cover.

Place in a moderate oven for 1½ hours. Add peeled and sliced potatoes half-way through the cooking time.

Savoury Baked Veal

Cooking time about 1½ hours
Oven temperature
375°F., 190°C., Gas Mark 5
Serves 4–6

Imperial/Metric	American
3-lb./1⅓-kg. piece boned leg of veal, the fillet end	3-lb. piece veal, rolled loin roast or tenderloin
1 level teaspoon chopped sage	1 teaspoon chopped sage
1 level teaspoon brown sugar	1 teaspoon brown sugar
1 level tablespoon dry mustard	1 tablespoon dry mustard
1 level teaspoon salt	1 teaspoon salt
3 tablespoons tarragon vinegar	4 tablespoons tarragon vinegar
4 rashers bacon	4 bacon slices

Get the butcher to tie boned joint into a neat shape for roasting. Put the meat, skin side up, in a deep casserole. Mix sage, sugar, mustard, salt and vinegar together. Pour over meat. Remove rinds and put bacon on top of meat. Cover with lid or aluminium foil.

Bake in a moderately hot oven for about 1½ hours or until tender, basting from time to time. Remove string before serving. Serve hot or cold, sliced thinly.

Poultry Dishes

Duckling Casserole

Cooking time about 2–2½ hours
Oven temperature
350°F., 180°C., Gas Mark 4 for 15 minutes
300°F., 150°C., Gas Mark 2 for 1½–2 hours
Serves 4

Imperial/Metric	American
1 duckling cut into four portions	1 duckling cut into four portions
salt and black pepper	salt and black pepper
2 onions	2 onions
1 bay leaf	1 bay leaf
½ pint/3 dl. red wine	1¼ cups red wine
4 oz./100 g. bacon	¼ lb. bacon
a little cooking oil	a little cooking oil
¼ pint/1½ dl. stock	⅔ cup stock
1 carrot	1 carrot
2 sticks celery	2 stalks celery
4 oz./100 g. button mushrooms	1 cup button mushrooms
grated orange rind	grated orange rind
chopped parsley	chopped parsley

Wipe the duckling with a damp cloth, sprinkle with salt and freshly ground black pepper. Peel, slice and chop onions, and place in a bowl with seasoned duckling and bay leaf. Pour over wine and leave to stand in a cool place for 2 hours. Remove the portions with a draining spoon; dry on absorbent paper. Reserve liquid.

Trim bacon, cut into pieces and cook in the oil gently for 3–4 minutes. Add duckling and brown all over in hot oil. Drain the duckling well, then place in an ovenproof casserole and cook in a moderate oven for 15 minutes. Remove from oven, pour over wine mixture and prepared stock. Peel and chop carrot, chop celery and rinse mushrooms; add to casserole. Cover and return to cool oven for a further 1½–2 hours or until tender. Remove excess fat with soft kitchen paper. Sprinkle with orange rind and parsley.

Roast Duckling with Apple and Orange Sauce

Cooking time approx. 1 hour 40 minutes
Oven temperature
350°F., 180°C., Gas Mark 4
Serves 4

Imperial/Metric	American
1 dressed duckling (about 4 lb./1¾ kg.)	1 duckling, about 4 lb., ready to cook
salt and pepper	salt and pepper
for sauce	**for sauce**
8 oz./225 g. cooking apples	½ lb. cooking apples
finely grated rind and juice of 1 large orange	finely grated rind and juice of 1 large orange
1 oz./25 g. butter	2 tablespoons butter
1 rounded tablespoon demerara sugar	1–2 tablespoons raw sugar
for gravy	**for gravy**
duckling giblets	duckling giblets
salt and pepper	salt and pepper
bay leaf	bay leaf
3 level tablespoons plain flour	4 tablespoons all-purpose flour
3 tablespoons water	4 tablespoons water
1 teaspoon vegetable extract	1 teaspoon vegetable flavoring extract
1 tablespoon chopped parsley	1 tablespoon chopped parsley

Sprinkle duckling with salt and pepper. Place in roasting pan and prick the skin well with a fork, cook in a moderate oven allowing 20 minutes to the lb./450 g. plus 20 minutes. Baste frequently. Garnish with slices of orange and watercress. Hand sauce and gravy separately.

To prepare apple and orange sauce
Peel apples, grate on coarse grater. Mix with orange rind and juice. Place butter in small saucepan, heat gently until just melted. Add apple and orange mixture and stir over gentle heat until smooth. Beat in sugar just before serving.

To prepare gravy
Cover duckling giblets with water. Season with salt and pepper, add bay leaf. Simmer for 1 hour. Blend flour, water, vegetable extract and parsley in small saucepan. Gradually blend in strained hot stock and cook, over gentle heat, stirring, for few minutes. Season if necessary.

Shown in colour on page 63

Roast Chicken with Country Stuffing

Cooking time about 1½ hours
Oven temperature
375°F., 190°C., Gas Mark 5
Serves 4

Imperial/Metric	American
1 dressed chicken (about 3 lb./1⅓ kg.)	3 lb. roasting chicken, ready to cook
2 oz./50 g. butter	¼ cup butter
for stuffing	**for stuffing**
2 oz./50 g. butter	¼ cup butter
1 onion, chopped	1 onion, chopped
2 celery sticks, chopped	2 celery stalks, chopped
4 oz./100 g. fresh white breadcrumbs	2 cups fresh soft white bread crumbs
finely grated rind of 1 lemon	finely grated rind of 1 lemon
1 tablespoon chopped parsley	1 tablespoon chopped parsley
salt and pepper	salt and pepper
a little beaten egg to bind	a little beaten egg to bind
for gravy	**for gravy**
sediment left in roasting pan	sediment left in roasting pan
1 level tablespoon plain flour	1 tablespoon all-purpose flour
1 pint/6 dl. chicken stock (made from giblets)	2½ cups chicken stock (made from giblets)
salt and pepper	salt and pepper

Prepare stuffing and stuff chicken. Weigh chicken and calculate the cooking time, allowing 20 minutes to the lb./450 g. and 20 minutes over. Stand chicken in roasting pan, spread with butter and cover with aluminium foil. Roast in a moderately hot oven for

calculated cooking time. Remove foil 15 minutes before end to allow for browning.

Make stuffing
Melt fat in saucepan, add onion and celery and cook gently for 5 minutes. Mix in breadcrumbs, lemon rind and parsley. Season to taste and bind with egg.

For gravy
Pour off fat from roasting pan leaving sediment and juices, blend in flour and cook for 2 or 3 minutes. Add stock gradually, stirring until smooth. Season to taste.

Chicken and Ham Croquettes

Cooking time 15 minutes
Serves 4

Imperial/Metric	American
1 oz./25 g. butter	2 tablespoons butter
1 oz./25 g. flour	¼ cup all-purpose flour
⅓ pint/2 dl. milk	generous ¾ cup milk
8 oz./225 g. cooked chicken, finely chopped	½ lb. cooked chicken, finely chopped
8 oz./225 g. ham, finely chopped	½ lb. ham, finely chopped
2 small red-skinned apples, cored and chopped	2 small red-skinned apples, cored and chopped
grated rind of 1 lemon	grated rind of 1 lemon
salt and pepper	salt and pepper
for coating and frying	**for coating and frying**
beaten egg	beaten egg
breadcrumbs	bread crumbs
fat for deep frying	fat for deep frying
for garnish	**for garnish**
parsley	parsley

Make a thick white sauce with the butter, flour and milk. Add the finely chopped meats, apple and lemon rind. Season to taste. Allow mixture to cool. Form into cork shapes, dust with flour and coat with beaten egg and breadcrumbs. Chill for 45 minutes. Deep fry about 10 minutes until golden. Drain on kitchen paper. Serve garnished with parsley.

Shown in colour on page 31

Crisp Fried Chicken with Piquant Brown Sauce

Cooking time about 50 minutes
Serves 4

Imperial/Metric	American
4 chicken joints	4 chicken joints
2 oz./50 g. flour	½ cup flour
1½ teaspoons dry mustard	1½ teaspoons dry mustard
1 teaspoon salt	1 teaspoon salt
¼ teaspoon freshly ground pepper	¼ teaspoon freshly milled pepper
2 oz./50 g. butter	¼ cup butter
2 oz./50 g. bacon dripping	¼ cup bacon drippings
for piquant brown sauce	**for piquant brown sauce**
1 oz./25 g. butter or bacon dripping	2 tablespoons butter or bacon drippings
1 oz./25 g. flour	¼ cup flour
1 teaspoon made-mustard	1 teaspoon made-mustard
1 teaspoon Worcestershire sauce	1 teaspoon Worcestershire sauce
¾ pint/4½ dl. chicken stock	scant 2 cups chicken stock
salt and pepper	salt and pepper

Coat chicken joints with seasoned flour, shaking one at a time in a paper bag. Melt butter and bacon fat and fry chicken joints slowly, turning to brown; cover and cook very gently for about 30 minutes. Uncover and cook for another 10 minutes, until crisp and brown.

Meanwhile, make sauce: melt fat in saucepan and blend in flour, cook, stirring until browned. Stir in mustard and Worcestershire sauce, then stock. Cook, stirring until thick and smooth. Season with salt and pepper.

Dorset Rabbit

Cooking time 2 hours 15 minutes
Oven temperature
350°F., 180°C., Gas Mark 4
Serves 4

Imperial/Metric	American
1 young rabbit, jointed	1 young rabbit, jointed
1 tablespoon seasoned flour	1 tablespoon seasoned flour
4 rashers fat bacon, trimmed	4 fat bacon slices, trimmed
2 tablespoons cider	2–3 tablespoons cider
for topping	**for topping**
8 oz./225 g. fresh white breadcrumbs	4 cups fresh soft white bread crumbs
4 oz./100 g. shredded suet	scant 1 cup finely chopped beef suet
2 large onions, finely chopped	2 large onions, finely chopped
2 teaspoons finely chopped or powdered sage	2 teaspoons finely chopped or powdered sage
grated rind of ½ small lemon	grated rind of ½ small lemon
1 beaten egg plus a little milk	1 beaten egg plus a little milk

Wash the rabbit and blanch (put in cold water, bring to boil and drain), pat dry in a clean cloth and toss in seasoned flour. Lay joints in a casserole, cover with bacon and pour over cider.

Mix topping ingredients together, adding sufficient milk to bind to a stuffing consistency. Cover rabbit with mixture, pressing down evenly with hand. Cover and bake in a moderate oven for 2 hours. Remove lid and cook for about 15 minutes longer to brown topping.

Rabbit and Bacon Pudding

Cooking time 4 hours
Serves 4

Imperial/Metric	American
8 oz./225 g. suet crust pastry (see page 44)	½ lb. suet crust (see page 44)
for filling	**for filling**
12 oz.–1 lb./350–450 g. jointed rabbit	¾–1 lb. jointed rabbit
8 oz./225 g. lean bacon collar (soaked overnight)	½ lb. Canadian bacon (soaked overnight)
2 onions, chopped	2 onions, chopped
2 cooking apples, chopped	2 cooking apples, chopped
salt and pepper	salt and pepper
cider or stock	cider or stock

Wash the rabbit and blanch (bring to boil in cold water and drain). Cut the bacon into cubes. Line a greased pudding basin with most of rolled out pastry, retaining just enough for the cover. Fill with layers of rabbit, bacon, onion and apple, seasoning each layer. Pour in cider or stock nearly to cover. Damp edges of pastry. Roll out rest of pastry for lid and place in position, press edges firmly together to seal. Use a sharp knife to trim edges neatly. Cover top closely with aluminium foil leaving room for pudding to swell.

Place in top of a steamer and steam steadily for 4 hours, refilling bottom pan as necessary. Remove foil from pudding. Arrange clean napkin round bowl for holding, and serve.

Puddings and Pies

Our unique contribution to European cooking is, without doubt, our delicious puddings and pies. Give a Frenchman, an Italian, or any other continental, a real home-baked apple pie with a dollop of fresh cream and he'll rave about it.

Most of the men in our lives nurture a secret longing for those massive puddings that for generations have kept our climate at bay: apple dumplings, spotted dog, suet puddings and all those wonderful 'afters' which are as British as the roast beef of Old England.

Here are a few tips to help you make *really light pastry*:

Weigh and measure ingredients carefully; it's most important to use the correct proportion of fat to flour.

Use plain flour, except in suet crust, and sift with salt into a good sized mixing bowl. Have the fat at room temperature. It must be firm but pliable; in no case allow it to 'oil'.

Use fingertips only to rub the fat into the flour, never use the palm of the hand. And lift the mixture in the air each time to introduce as much air as possible.

Add the liquid carefully as the amount given in the recipe can only be a guide, it will vary with the type of flour and fat used. Too little water makes the pastry difficult to handle because of cracks, too much water makes it tough and hard when it is cooked.

Don't over-handle the dough. Roll briskly and firmly in one direction only, using only a little flour for dredging the board.

Bake pastry quickly in a moderately hot to hot oven.

Note
When quantities of pastry are given in this book the amount indicates the weight of flour used in recipe; increase or decrease other ingredients accordingly, i.e. for 4 oz./110 g. pastry use 4 oz./110 g. flour, etc.

To bake 'blind'
(this prevents pastry rising during cooking when making flan, tart or pie cases)

If making a flan, then stand the flan ring on a baking sheet first. Line the flan ring, tart or pie plate with rolled out pastry, press down to fit, trim edge. Prick base lightly with a fork. Line the inside with a square of greaseproof paper and weigh it down with rice or dried beans. Bake in a moderately hot oven (375°F., 190°C., Gas Mark 5) for 15 minutes to set the pastry. Remove paper and rice or beans and return flan to oven for further 10 minutes, or until cooked.

Note
Rice or beans can be stored in a screw-top jar and used again.

Pastry Making

Short Crust Pastry

Makes 8 oz./225 g. short crust pastry
(½ lb. basic pie dough)

Imperial/Metric	American
8 oz./225 g. plain flour	2 cups all-purpose flour
pinch of salt	pinch of salt
2 oz./50 g. butter or margarine	¼ cup butter or margarine
2 oz./50 g. lard or cooking fat	¼ cup lard or shortening
approx. 3 tablespoons cold water	approx. 4 tablespoons cold water

Sift the flour and salt into a bowl, add fats and cut into flour with a knife. Use fingertips to rub in fat lightly until mixture looks like fine breadcrumbs. Stir water in with a knife, then draw mixture together with fingers to form a firm but pliable dough. Knead gently on a lightly floured board until free from cracks.

Rich Short Crust Pastry

Makes 8 oz./225 g. rich short crust pastry
(½ lb. rich pie dough)

Imperial/Metric	American
8 oz./225 g. plain flour	2 cups all-purpose flour
pinch of salt	pinch of salt
4 oz./110 g. butter or margarine	½ cup butter or margarine
1 egg yolk	1 egg yolk
1–1½ tablespoons cold water	about 2 tablespoons cold water

Sift the flour with salt into a bowl, add fat and cut into flour with a knife. Use fingertips to rub in fat lightly until mixture looks like fine breadcrumbs. Mix the egg yolk with the water, tip into flour and fat mixture and work to a firm dough. Turn on to a lightly floured board and knead lightly until smooth.

Note

For sweet dishes add 2 teaspoons castor sugar after rubbing fat into flour.

Flaky Pastry

Makes 8 oz./225 g. flaky pastry
(½ lb. rich flaky pie dough)

Imperial/Metric	American
8 oz./225 g. plain flour	2 cups all-purpose flour
pinch of salt	pinch of salt
6 oz./175 g. butter or margarine	¾ cup butter or margarine
scant ¼ pint/1½ dl. cold water	scant ⅔ cup cold water

Sieve the flour with salt into a bowl. Divide fat into three portions. Rub one portion of fat lightly into flour. Use sufficient cold water to mix to rolling consistency. Roll out dough to oblong shape. Take the second portion of fat, divide it into small pieces and lay them on the surface of two-thirds of the dough. Leave the remaining third without fat, take its two corners and fold back over second third so that the dough looks like an envelope with its flap open. Fold over top end of pastry, so closing the 'envelope'. Turn pastry at right angles, seal open ends of pastry and 'rib' it (this means gently depress it at intervals to give a corrugated effect); this distributes the air and helps pastry to rise evenly. Repeat the process again using the remaining fat and turning pastry in same way. Roll out pastry once more, but should it begin to feel very soft and sticky put in a cold place for 30 minutes before rolling out.

Fold pastry as before, turn it, seal edges and 'rib' it. Altogether the pastry should have three foldings and three turnings. It is then ready to stand in a cold place before using.

Suet Crust Pastry

Makes 8 oz./225 g. suet crust pastry
(½ lb. suet crust)

Imperial/Metric	American
8 oz./225 g. self-raising flour	2 cups all-purpose flour, sifted with 2 teaspoons double-acting baking powder
pinch of salt	pinch of salt
4 oz./110 g. shredded suet	¾ cup finely chopped beef suet
cold water to mix	cold water to mix

Sift the flour and salt into a bowl, mix in the suet. Add sufficient cold water to mix to a firm dough. Knead lightly on a floured board.

Pudding Recipes

Creamy Rice Pudding

Cooking time 2–3 hours
Oven temperature
300°F., 150°C., Gas Mark 2
Serves 4

Imperial/Metric	American
1½ oz./40 g. Carolina rice	¼ cup raw rice, short-grain
1½ oz./40 g. sugar	3 tablespoons granulated sugar
1 pint/6 dl. milk	2½ cups milk
½ oz./15 g. butter	1 tablespoon butter

Wash the rice in cold water. Put in a greased pie dish with the other ingredients. Stir well. Cook low down in a cool oven for 2 or 3 hours. After about 30 minutes you can stir in the skin; this helps to make an extra-creamy pudding.

Queen of Puddings

Cooking time about 40 minutes
Oven temperature
375°F., 190°C., Gas Mark 5 for 30 minutes
350°F., 180°C., Gas Mark 4 for 10 minutes
Serves 4

Imperial/Metric	American
½ pint/3 dl. milk	1¼ cups milk
peeled rind of 1 small lemon	peeled rind of 1 small lemon
½ oz./15 g. butter	1 tablespoon butter
1 oz./25 g. castor sugar	2 tablespoons granulated sugar
2 oz./50 g. fresh white breadcrumbs	1 cup fresh soft white bread crumbs
2 egg yolks	2 egg yolks
2–3 tablespoons strawberry or raspberry jam	3–4 tablespoons strawberry or raspberry jam
for meringue topping	**for meringue topping**
2 egg whites	2 egg whites
4 oz./100 g. castor sugar	½ cup granulated sugar or ⅔ cup powdered sugar

Heat the milk very gently with the lemon rind, then leave in the covered pan for few minutes. Strain into a bowl, add the butter and sugar and, when dissolved, the breadcrumbs. Mix and leave to cool. Stir in the egg yolks, mix well together and turn into a lightly greased pie dish. Stand 30 minutes, then bake in a moderately hot oven for 25–30 minutes until set. Remove from oven, cool slightly; spread top with jam.

Whisk egg whites until very stiff, add 2 teaspoons of sugar and whisk until satiny-looking, fold in rest of sugar. Pile meringue on top and put back in a moderate oven for 10 minutes until lightly browned.

Castle Puddings

Cooking time 15 minutes
Oven temperature
375°F., 190°C., Gas Mark 5
Serves 4

Imperial/Metric	American
4 oz./110 g. butter or margarine	½ cup butter or margarine
4 oz./110 g. castor sugar	½ cup granulated sugar
2 eggs	2 eggs
4 oz./110 g. self-raising flour	1 cup all-purpose flour, sifted with 1 teaspoon double-acting baking powder
for jam sauce	**for jam sauce**
4 tablespoons raspberry jam heated with 1 tablespoon water	5 tablespoons raspberry jam heated with 1–2 tablespoons water

Well grease eight dariole moulds. Cream the fat and sugar together until soft and fluffy. Beat in eggs, one at a time. Fold in the sifted flour. Half fill prepared moulds and place on a baking sheet. Bake in a moderately hot oven for 15 minutes, or until golden brown. Turn out on a hot dish and serve with jam sauce.

Brown Betty Pudding

Cooking time 1–1½ hours
Oven temperature
325°F., 170°C., Gas Mark 3
Serves 4

Imperial/Metric	American
6 oz./175 g. fine white breadcrumbs	3 cups fresh soft white bread crumbs
2 lb./900 g. cooking apples, peeled, cored and sliced	2 lb. cooking apples, pared, cored and sliced
1 lemon	1 lemon
4 tablespoons golden syrup	5 tablespoons corn syrup
4 oz./100 g. demerara sugar	½ cup raw sugar, firmly packed
¼ pint/1½ dl. water	⅔ cup water

Grease a 2-pint/1-litre pie dish or casserole and coat it with a layer of breadcrumbs. Fill the pie dish with alternate layers of apples, grated lemon rind and breadcrumbs. Heat the syrup, sugar and water in a pan, add the lemon juice and pour over the mixture. Bake in a very moderate oven for 1–1½ hours until browned.

Spotted Dick

Cooking time 2–2½ hours
Serves 4

Imperial/Metric	American
8 oz./225 g. plain flour	2 cups all-purpose flour
2 rounded teaspoons baking powder	3 teaspoons double-acting baking powder
2 oz./50 g. sugar	¼ cup sugar
3 oz./75 g. shredded suet	⅔ cup finely chopped beef suet
4 oz./100 g. currants	¾ cup currants
milk or milk and water to mix	milk or milk and water to mix
to serve	**to serve**
brown sugar	brown sugar
custard	custard

Mix together the flour, baking powder and sugar. Add the shredded suet and cleaned currants and mix with milk to a medium stiff dough, not too soft. Shape into a roll on a board, wrap a strip of greased paper round it, tie in a cloth like a sausage, leaving room for expansion. Boil for 2–2½ hours. Remove paper and cloth. Serve with brown sugar and custard.

Marmalade Suet Pudding

Cooking time 2–2½ hours
Serves 4

Imperial/Metric	American
4 oz./110 g. plain flour	1 cup all-purpose flour
½ teaspoon salt	½ teaspoon salt
2 teaspoons baking powder or 1 teaspoon bicarbonate of soda	2 teaspoons double-acting baking powder or 1 teaspoon baking soda
4 oz./110 g. fresh white breadcrumbs	2 cups fresh soft white bread crumbs
4 oz./110 g. shredded suet	¾ cup finely chopped beef suet
4 oz./110 g. sugar	½ cup sugar
2–3 tablespoons marmalade	3–4 tablespoons marmalade
1 egg	1 egg
¼ pint/1½ dl. milk	⅔ cup milk
for sauce	**for sauce**
3 tablespoons marmalade	4 tablespoons marmalade
3 tablespoons sugar	4 tablespoons sugar
¼ pint/1½ dl. water	⅔ cup water
grated rind and juice of ½ lemon	grated rind and juice of ½ lemon

Grease a 1½-pint/1-litre pudding basin. Sieve the flour, salt and baking powder into a basin and add breadcrumbs, shredded suet, sugar and marmalade. Beat the egg and add milk to it. Add the egg and milk to the mixture. Mix with a wooden spoon until well blended and a soft consistency. Two-thirds fill the greased basin. Cover with greased greaseproof paper

Old-fashioned Bread Pudding

or aluminium foil. Steam for 2–2½ hours. Turn out on a serving dish.

For sauce
Put all the ingredients into a saucepan and heat, stirring until sugar is dissolved.

Old-Fashioned Bread Pudding

Cooking time 1½ hours
Oven temperature
375°F., 190°C., Gas Mark 5
Serves 4

Imperial/Metric	American
9–10 slices stale bread	9–10 slices stale bread
5 oz./150 g. mixed dried fruit	1 cup mixed dried fruit
1 oz./25 g. mixed peel	3 tablespoons mixed candied peel
3 oz./75 g. soft brown sugar	⅓ cup brown sugar, firmly packed
4 teaspoons mixed spice	4 teaspoons mixed spices
2 oz./50 g. soft butter or margarine	¼ cup soft butter or margarine
castor sugar for sprinkling	powdered sugar for dredging

Grease a 7-inch/18-cm. round cake pan or 6-inch/15-cm. square pan or ovenproof dish. Soak the bread in cold water for at least 30 minutes. Squeeze the bread by hand or in a sieve to expel as much water as possible, then beat with a fork to remove any lumps. Add the remaining ingredients and mix thoroughly. Put the mixture into the greased pan or dish and bake in a moderately hot oven for about 1½ hours.

Sprinkle liberally with castor sugar and serve hot with custard, or cold with cream.

Bread and Butter Pudding

Cooking time 30–40 minutes
Oven temperature
350°F., 180°C., Gas Mark 4
Serves 4

Imperial/Metric	American
4 or 5 small slices of bread and butter, with crusts removed	4 or 5 small slices of bread and butter, with crusts removed
1½ oz./40 g. cleaned currants	4 tablespoons currants
1 egg	1 egg
½ oz./15 g. castor sugar	1 tablespoon granulated sugar
½ pint/3 dl. milk	1¼ cups milk

Cut the buttered bread into small pieces and place in a greased pie dish with currants sprinkled between the layers. Beat the egg, sugar and milk together with a fork and pour over the bread. Leave to stand for 15 minutes. Bake in a moderate oven for 30–40 minutes.

Junket

Cooking time 5 minutes
Serves 4

Imperial/Metric	American
1 pint/6 dl. milk	2½ cups milk
2 level teaspoons castor sugar	2 teaspoons granulated or powdered sugar
2 teaspoons essence of rennet	2 teaspoons essence of rennet or 1 teaspoon prepared rennet

Put the milk into a saucepan with the castor sugar and stir it over a gentle heat until it is at blood-heat. Pour the milk into a deep dish or bowl and thoroughly stir in the rennet. Leave it to set in a warm place – it will take only a few minutes.
Serve with stewed fruit and cream.

Fruit Fool

Cooking time 25 minutes
Serves 4

Imperial/Metric	American
1 lb./450 g. fruit (gooseberries, raspberries, etc.)	1 lb. fruit (gooseberries, raspberries, etc.)
¼ pint/1½ dl. water	⅔ cup water
4 oz./100 g. castor sugar	½ cup granulated sugar
¼ pint/1½ dl. double cream	⅔ cup whipping cream
¼ pint/1½ dl. cold custard (same consistency as the cream)	⅔ cup cold custard (same consistency as the cream)
ratafia biscuits	ratafias or lady fingers

Stew the fruit gently with the water and sugar. Sieve finely and leave to cool. Whip the double cream until thick and put a little aside for decoration. Fold into the custard. Stir in the cold sieved fruit. Put into individual dishes and chill well.

Decorate with remaining cream and serve with ratafia biscuits.

Fruit Sponge Cups

Cooking time about 30 minutes
Serves 6

Imperial/Metric	American
6 oz./175 g. self-raising flour	1½ cups all-purpose flour sifted with 1½ teaspoons double-acting baking powder
pinch of salt	pinch of salt
4 oz./110 g. butter or margarine	½ cup butter or margarine
5 oz./140 g. castor sugar	⅔ cup granulated sugar
2 eggs	2 eggs
2 tablespoons milk	2–3 tablespoons milk
4 oz./110 g. blackcurrants or redcurrants	1 cup black or red currants

Well grease six old tea cups or small moulds of just under ¼-pint/1½-dl. capacity, and put a circle of greased greaseproof paper in the bottom of each. Sift the flour and salt. Cream butter or margarine and 4 oz./110 g. sugar together until light and fluffy. Beat in eggs gradually, adding one tablespoon of flour with last amount of egg. Fold in remaining flour, and finally the milk. Mix remaining sugar with black- or redcurrants and place in bottom of cups or moulds.

Divide sponge mixture between cups on top of black- or redcurrants. Cover with greased foil or a double layer of greased greaseproof paper. Steam for about 30 minutes. Turn out and serve with whipped cream.

Fruit Sponge Cups

Apple Charlotte

Cooking time 50–60 minutes
Oven temperature
350°F., 180°C., Gas Mark 4
Serves 4

Imperial/Metric	American
6 oz./175 g. fine white breadcrumbs	3 cups fresh soft white bread crumbs
4 oz./110 g. shredded suet	¾ cup finely chopped beef suet
2 oz./50 g. granulated sugar	¼ cup sugar
for fruit mixture	**for fruit mixture**
1½ oz./40 g. butter	3 tablespoons butter
2 tablespoons water	3 tablespoons water
1½ lb./675 g. cooking apples, peeled, cored and diced	1½ lb. cooking apples, pared, cored and diced
3 oz./75 g. brown sugar	⅓ cup brown sugar
1 oz./25 g. sultanas or seedless raisins	3 tablespoons seedless white raisins
¼ level teaspoon cinnamon or mixed spice	¼ teaspoon cinnamon or mixed spices

Heavily grease a 2-pint/1-litre pie dish. Mix the breadcrumbs, suet and sugar well together, and press three-quarters of it on to bottom and sides of the dish.

Melt 1 oz./25 g. butter in a pan, add the water and apples. Cover and heat gently, shaking and stirring occasionally, until apples are well glazed but not too soft. Remove from heat, stir in 2 oz./50 g. brown sugar, sultanas and cinnamon. Pour into the prepared pie dish then top with remaining crumb mixture, pressing down neatly. Wipe edge of dish, then sprinkle crumbs with rest of brown sugar and dot with remaining butter. Bake in the centre of moderate oven for 50–60 minutes until golden brown.

Poor Knights of Windsor

Cooking time 10 minutes
Serves 4

Imperial/Metric	American
8 very thin slices bread	8 very thin slices bread
2 eggs	2 eggs
2 tablespoons milk	3 tablespoons milk
2 tablespoons sugar	3 tablespoons sugar
½ teaspoon vanilla essence	½ teaspoon vanilla extract
2 oz./50 g. butter	¼ cup butter
jam or lemon juice	jam or lemon juice
icing sugar	confectioners' sugar
to serve	**to serve**
whipped cream	whipped cream

Remove the crusts from the bread. Beat the eggs and pour on to a dinner plate, stir in the milk, sugar and vanilla essence and mix well together. Melt the butter in a frying pan and heat without browning. Dip the slices of bread into the egg mixture, just coating them on both sides, and fry on both sides until golden brown. Spread with jam and roll up. Secure with wooden cocktail sticks until set. Dust with icing sugar. Serve hot with whipped cream.

Pastry Recipes

Old-Fashioned Custard Tart

Cooking time approx. 1 hour
Oven temperature
375°F., 190°C., Gas Mark 5 for 30 minutes
300°F., 150°C., Gas Mark 2 for 30 minutes
Serves 4

Imperial/Metric	American
6 oz./175 g. short crust pastry (see page 44)	6 oz. basic pie dough (see page 44)
for filling	**for filling**
2–3 oz./50–75 g. chopped mixed peel	½ cup chopped mixed candied peel
½ pint/3 dl. lukewarm milk	1¼ cups lukewarm milk
2 beaten eggs	2 beaten eggs
1 oz./25 g. castor sugar	2 tablespoons granulated sugar
powdered cinnamon	powdered cinnamon

Roll pastry out on a lightly floured board to a 12-inch/30-cm. round and use it to line a deep 9-inch/23-cm. pie plate. Cover base evenly with peel. Pour milk over eggs and sugar and stir well. Strain into pastry-lined pie plate. Sprinkle top with cinnamon and bake for 30 minutes in a moderately hot oven, then in a cool oven for approximately a further 30 minutes, until pastry is golden and the custard set. Serve hot or cold.

Blackberry and Apple Tart

Cooking time 45–50 minutes
Oven temperature
425°F., 220°C., Gas Mark 7 for 10 minutes
350°F., 180°C., Gas Mark 4 for 35–40 minutes
Serves 4

Imperial/Metric	American
8 oz./225 g. short crust pastry (see page 44)	½ lb. basic pie dough (see page 44)
for filling	**for filling**
12 oz./350 g. peeled, cored and thinly sliced cooking apples	¾ lb. pared, cored and thinly sliced cooking apples
8 oz./225 g. blackberries	½ lb. blackberries
4 oz./100 g. castor sugar	½ cup granulated sugar
for egg wash	**for egg glaze**
1 egg, beaten with 2 tablespoons water and 1 teaspoon sugar	1 egg, beaten with 3 tablespoons water and 1 teaspoon sugar

Turn the pastry on to a floured board. Roll out two-thirds and with it line an 8-inch/20-cm. pie plate. Fill with apples, blackberries and sugar to taste. Roll out rest of pastry, moisten edges and cover pie. Press edges well together to seal and decorate. Brush with egg wash. Bake towards top of a hot oven for 10 minutes, then in a moderate oven for 35–40 minutes.

Apple Plate Pie

Cooking time about 50 minutes
Oven temperature
400°F., 200°C., Gas Mark 6
Serves 4

Imperial/Metric	American
12 oz./350 g. short crust pastry (see page 44)	¾ lb. basic pie dough (see page 44)
for filling	**for filling**
1½ lb./675 g. cooking apples, peeled, cored and sliced	1½ lb. cooking apples, pared, cored and sliced
8 oz./225 g. granulated sugar	1 cup granulated sugar
1 clove	1 clove
for glaze	**for glaze**
egg white or milk	egg white or milk
castor sugar	granulated sugar

Gently stew the apples with sugar, clove and very little water in a covered pan until tender, about 20 minutes. Allow to cool before using.

Roll out the pastry on a lightly floured board. Cut into two circles to fit a 9-inch/23-cm. pie plate, making one circle slightly larger than the other. Lift the smaller circle on to pie plate, press down and put in prepared filling. Damp edges and cover with other circle. Seal

edges, trim and flute. Make three small cuts across centre. Brush top with egg white or milk and sprinkle with castor sugar. Stand pie on baking sheet and bake in a hot oven for about 30 minutes.

Apple Dumplings

Cooking time about 1 hour
Oven temperature
425°F., 220°C., Gas Mark 7 for 20 minutes
375°F., 190°C., Gas Mark 5 for 40 minutes
Serves 4

Imperial/Metric	American
4 small cooking apples	4 small cooking apples
1 oz./25 g. brown sugar	3 tablespoons brown sugar
½ oz./15 g. dates or 4 cloves	2 tablespoons chopped pitted dates or 4 cloves
1 lb./450 g. short crust pastry (see page 44)	1 lb. basic pie dough (see page 44)
egg beaten with a little water	egg beaten with a little water

Peel and core the apples and stuff the middles with the sugar and chopped dates or a clove. Roll out the pastry to ¼-inch/1-cm. thickness, cut into four rounds large enough to enclose the apples. Place each apple in the centre of a pastry round, wet the edges and fold up round the apple, flattening the creases as much as possible. From trimmings cut three ¼ inch/1 cm. wide strips, 6 inches/15 cm. long, and plait.

Brush dumplings with egg wash, place plait over top and brush again. Bake in a hot oven until the pastry has set and begins to brown (about 20 minutes), then reduce heat and continue to bake more slowly in a moderately hot oven, covering if necessary to prevent over-browning, until the apples are quite cooked (about 40 minutes).

Rhubarb and Orange Tart

Cooking time about 30 minutes
Oven temperature
400°F., 200°C., Gas Mark 6
Serves 4

Imperial/Metric	American
8 oz./225 g. short crust pastry (see page 44)	½ lb. basic pie dough (see page 44)
for filling	**for filling**
1 lb./450 g. early rhubarb	1 lb. young rhubarb
6 oz./175 g. sugar	¾ cup granulated sugar
1 oz./25 g. flour	¼ cup all-purpose flour
1 beaten egg	1 beaten egg
grated rind of 1 orange	grated rind of 1 orange
2 tablespoons orange juice made to ¼ pint/1½ dl. with water	3 tablespoons orange juice made to ⅔ cup with water

Roll out the pastry on a lightly floured board and line an 8-inch/20-cm. ovenproof plate, saving the trimmings for lattice. Wipe the rhubarb and cut into 1-inch/3-cm. lengths and place in pastry case. In a basin blend together sugar, flour, egg and rind of orange. Place juice and water in a pan and bring to the boil. Pour on to flour mixture, stir briskly. Return to the pan and bring to the boil, stirring all the time. Pour over rhubarb. Cut strips from trimmings and place on filling to form a lattice.

Bake for about 30 minutes. Serve hot or cold.

Elizabethan Flan

Cooking time about 55 minutes
Oven temperature
375°F., 190°C., Gas Mark 5
Serves 4

Imperial/Metric	American
8 oz./225 g. rich short crust pastry (see page 44)	½ lb. rich pie dough (see page 44)
for filling	**for filling**
2 large thin-skinned oranges	2 large thin-skinned oranges
2 tablespoons honey	3 tablespoons honey
¼ pint/1½ dl. water	⅔ cup water
¼ pint/1½ dl. double cream	⅔ cup whipping cream
2 oz./50 g. granulated sugar	¼ cup granulated sugar

Wash the oranges and cut into thin rings, the peel should be kept on. Soak overnight in honey and water. Next day, place oranges and liquid in pan and simmer for 25–30 minutes. Drain and cook, reserve syrup. Stand an 8-inch/20-cm. flan ring on a baking sheet and line with rolled out pastry, trim edges. Bake 'blind' (see page 43) in moderately hot oven for 15 minutes.

Elizabethan Flan

Remove paper and filling and cook for further 10 minutes or until pale golden. Cool.
Whip cream until just stiff and spread over bottom of flan case. Overlap orange slices on top. Add sugar to ¼ pint/1½ dl. honey liquid and heat gently until sugar has dissolved. Bring to boil and cook until syrupy consistency, 3–5 minutes. Use this to glaze oranges. Serve chilled.

Favourite Plum Pie

Cooking time 40 minutes
Oven temperature
400°F., 200°C., Gas Mark 6
Serves 4

Imperial/Metric	American
12 oz./350 g. short crust pastry (see page 44)	¾ lb. basic pie dough (see page 44)
for filling	**for filling**
2 lb./900 g. plums	2 lb. plums
8 oz./225 g. demerara sugar	1 cup raw sugar, firmly packed
finely grated rind of 1 lemon	finely grated rind of 1 lemon
5 tablespoons water	6 tablespoons water
for topping	**for topping**
castor sugar	granulated sugar

Put washed fruit in a deep pie dish, sprinkle sugar and lemon rind between layers. Put a pie funnel in centre. Add water. Roll out pastry on lightly floured board into an oval slightly larger than pie top; cut strip from edge and use to line damped rim of pie dish, damp this strip and cover pie with rest of pastry. Trim, rough up and flute edges.
Make a small air vent in top. Stand pie on a baking sheet and cook in a hot oven for about 40 minutes. Dredge the top with castor sugar.

Creamy pear flan, page 52

Pear Pie

Cooking time 30 minutes
Oven temperature
400°F., 200°C., Gas Mark 6
Serves 4

Imperial/Metric	American
12 oz./350 g. short crust pastry (see page 44)	¾ lb. basic pie dough (see page 44)
for filling	**for filling**
2 lb./900 g. medium ripe pears, peeled, cored and halved	2 lb. medium ripe pears, pared, cored and halved
juice of 1 lemon	juice of 1 lemon
piece of cinnamon stick	piece of cinnamon stick
3 tablespoons heated apricot jam	4 tablespoons heated apricot jelly
2 oz./50 g. sugar	¼ cup granulated sugar
2 tablespoons water	3 tablespoons water
for topping	**for topping**
castor sugar	granulated sugar

Toss the pear halves lightly in lemon juice, leave to stand 10 minutes. Place pear halves in a deep pie dish, add cinnamon stick, apricot jam and sugar. Put a pie funnel in centre. Add water.

Roll out pastry on a lightly floured board into an oval, slightly larger than pie top, cut strip from edge and use to line damped rim of pie dish; damp this strip and cover pie with rest of pastry. Trim, rough up and flute edges. Make a small air vent in the top. Stand pie on a baking sheet and cook in hot oven for about 30 minutes. Dredge the top with castor sugar.

Creamy Pear Flan

Cooking time 1 hour
Oven temperature
375°F., 190°C., Gas Mark 5
Serves 4

Imperial/Metric	American
8 oz./225 g. rich short crust pastry (see page 44)	½ lb. rich pie dough (see page 44)
for filling	**for filling**
3 small peeled, cored and halved pears	3 small pared, cored and halved pears
¼ pint/1½ dl. double cream	⅔ cup whipping cream
2 oz./50 g. sugar	¼ cup granulated sugar
1 teaspoon vanilla essence	1 teaspoon vanilla extract

Line a flan case with the pastry. Prick base with a fork and bake 'blind' (see page 43) for 10 minutes. Remove filling and cool slightly.

Arrange pears in base of the flan. Blend the cream, sugar and vanilla essence and pour over pears. Bake in a moderately hot oven for about 40 minutes. Serve hot or cold.

Shown in colour on page 51

Farmhouse Bread and Tea Bakes

For those of us who have country memories there is surely one that has special meaning: the wonderful warm and welcoming smell of baking. In this country, baking is still a special pride and craft and there is still no lack of competition to display cakes and bakes at local fêtes.

Baking bread is a specially satisfying and rewarding task and the recipes I've included are not difficult to make.

If you find it difficult to buy fresh yeast, then dried yeast is an excellent substitute; sold in tins of various sizes it keeps well for up to six months in a cool place.

After the dough has been kneaded it is 'put to rise' which means left on one side until it swells and doubles its size. For a quick rise leave it in a warm place for 45–60 minutes, for a slower rise leave it for 2 hours at average room temperature.

It is then shaped into loaves and 'put to prove' (allowed to rise again) for about 20–30 minutes. Be careful not to over-prove the mixture or you'll lose the shape of the dough. Bake the bread in a very hot oven until deep golden brown and crusty – when it's cooked, the bread should sound hollow if you tap the base with your knuckles. Bread takes a short time to mix and a long time to rise, so organise the rising time to suit yourself.

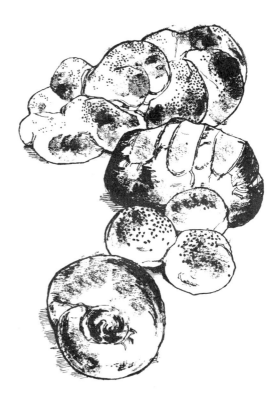

Cottage Loaves

Cooking time 25–35 minutes
Oven temperature
450°F., 230°C., Gas Mark 8
Makes 2 loaves

Imperial/Metric	American
2 lb./900 g. plain flour	8 cups all-purpose flour
2 level teaspoons sugar	2 teaspoons sugar
4 level teaspoons dried yeast	2 packages active dry yeast
16 fl. oz./4 dl. lukewarm milk	2 cups lukewarm milk
2 standard eggs	2 eggs
6 tablespoons cooking oil	½ cup cooking oil
2 level teaspoons salt	2 teaspoons salt

Sift 10 oz./250 g. of the flour into a mixing bowl. Add sugar, yeast and lukewarm (NOT hot) milk. Mix well, then leave in a warm place for about 20 minutes until frothy. Add beaten eggs, oil, remaining sifted flour and salt. Beat well.

Turn dough on to a lightly floured board and knead and stretch well for 10 minutes until the dough is elastic and no longer sticky. Shape the dough into a neat round and place in an oiled polythene bag. Loosely tie the bag and place in a bowl. Allow to rise in a warm place for 45–60 minutes, longer in a cool one, until the dough is double its size and springs back when pressed with a finger.

Turn dough on to a board, flatten firmly to knock out any air bubbles. Knead lightly, then divide into two. Cut off a third of the dough from each. Shape the larger piece into a neat round and place on a greased baking tray. Shape the remaining piece into a slightly smaller round and place on top.

Press the handle of a wooden spoon right through the centre of the loaves. Cover with a damp cloth, then leave to prove in a warm place for 20–30 minutes. Dust loaves with flour and bake on centre shelf of a very hot oven for approximately 25–35 minutes until golden brown and crusty. When cooked, the loaves should sound hollow if tapped on base. Place on wire rack and cool.

Quick Wheatmeal Bread

Cooking time 30–40 minutes
Oven temperature
450°F., 230°C., Gas Mark 8
Makes 1 loaf (9 inches/22½ cm.) and 3 rolls

Imperial/Metric	American
½ oz./15 g. fresh yeast or	½ oz. fresh yeast or
2 level teaspoons dried yeast	1 package active dry yeast
1 lb./400 g. mixed plain flours, wholemeal and white in any proportion you like	4 cups mixed all-purpose and wholewheat flours in any proportion you like
2 teaspoons each salt and sugar	2 teaspoons each salt and sugar
½ pint/2½ dl. water	1¼ cups water

Using fresh yeast
Rub yeast into flour, salt and sugar, add all the water and mix to a soft dough, using your hand or a wooden spoon. Work to a smooth dough, adding more flour if needed, until the dough leaves sides of the basin clean.

Using dried yeast
Add a teaspoon of sugar to a cup of the water used in recipe (to get best results the water should be warmed to 110°F./45°C., or hand-hot). Sprinkle the dried yeast on top. Leave until frothy – about 10 minutes. Add to the flour, salt and remaining sugar with rest of liquid, dough up and knead thoroughly on a floured board.

To make loaves
(makes 1 1-lb./400-g. loaf and 3 2-oz./50-g. rolls)
Half fill well greased 1-lb./400-g. loaf pan with dough. Put inside a large greased polythene bag, loosely tied, and allow to rise to double size, 45–60 minutes in a warm place, longer in a cool one. Remove bag. Bake on middle shelf of a very hot oven for 30–40 minutes. Turn out on a wire rack and cool.

Pear pie, page 52
Hunter's rolls, page 58

Harvest Loaf

board and knead until dough is smooth (about 10 minutes). Leave to rise in a bowl covered with a lid or lightly greased polythene bag until double in size, about 45–60 minutes in a warm place, longer in a cool one.

Punch dough well to knock out any large air bubbles. Divide into four pieces. Roll three of the pieces into 20-inch/50-cm. long strands and join together at one end. Place on a lightly greased baking sheet and plait loosely together; tuck ends underneath. Brush with egg wash. Divide fourth piece into two and roll each to a 20-inch/50-cm. long strand. Join together at one end and twist strands loosely. Lay twist along centre of plait and tuck ends underneath.

Brush twist with egg wash. Leave to rise at room temperature, covered with greased polythene, until dough springs back when pressed lightly, about 30 minutes. Bake in a very hot oven for 30–40 minutes.

For egg wash
Beat the egg and pinch of sugar with a little water.

Harvest Loaf

Cooking time 30–40 minutes
Oven temperature
450°F., 230°C., Gas Mark 8
Makes 1 loaf (9 inches/22½ cm.)

Imperial/Metric	American
½ oz./15 g. fresh yeast or	½ oz. fresh yeast or
2 level teaspoons dried yeast	1 package active dry yeast
½ pint less 2 tablespoons/2½ dl. warm water	1 cup plus 2 tablespoons warm water
1 lb./400 g. plain flour	4 cups all-purpose flour
2 level teaspoons salt	2 teaspoons salt
½ oz./15 g. lard	1 tablespoon lard
for egg wash	**for egg wash**
1 egg	1 egg
pinch of sugar	pinch of sugar

For yeast liquid
Blend ½ oz./15 g. fresh yeast in ½ pint less 2 tablespoons/2½ dl. warm water *OR* dissolve 1 teaspoon sugar in ½ pint less 2 tablespoons/2½ dl. warm water, sprinkle on 2 level teaspoons dried yeast and leave until frothy – about 10 minutes.

To make loaf
Mix the flour and salt in a bowl, rub in lard. Add the yeast liquid all at once and mix to a firm dough, adding extra flour if needed until dough leaves the sides of the bowl clean. Turn on to a lightly floured

Date Loaf

Cooking time 1¼–1½ hours
Oven temperature
300°F., 150°C., Gas Mark 2
Makes 1 loaf

Imperial/Metric	American
8 oz./225 g. plain flour	2 cups all-purpose flour
1 level teaspoon bicarbonate of soda	1 teaspoon baking soda
8 oz./225 g. stoned dates	2 cups chopped pitted dates
¼ pint/1½ dl. water	⅔ cup water
3 oz./75 g. butter or margarine	6 tablespoons butter or margarine
1 egg	1 egg

Grease and line a 2-lb./1-kg. loaf pan with greased greaseproof paper. Sift the flour with the bicarbonate of soda. Finely chop the dates and place in a small saucepan with the water. Heat together until soft. Remove from heat and beat well with a wooden spoon until smooth. Mix in the butter or margarine and allow to cool for 5 minutes.

Stir in the beaten egg then beat in flour mixture. Pour into prepared pan and bake in a cool oven for 1¼–1½ hours or until spongy to touch. Turn on to a wire tray, remove paper and leave to cool. Store two days in an airtight tin before cutting. Serve in slices spread with butter.

Glazed Cherry Bread

Cooking time 1 hour 5 minutes
Oven temperature
325°F., 170°C., Gas Mark 3
Makes 2 loaves

Imperial/Metric	American
12 oz./350 g. self-raising flour	3 cups all-purpose flour, sifted with 3 teaspoons double-acting baking powder
1 teaspoon salt	1 teaspoon salt
2 oz./50 g. castor sugar	¼ cup granulated sugar
2 oz./50 g. walnuts, chopped	½ cup chopped walnuts
2 oz./50 g. dates, stoned and chopped	½ cup chopped pitted dates
2 rounded tablespoons malt extract	3 tablespoons malt extract
2 oz./50 g. butter or margarine	¼ cup butter or margarine
¼ pint/1½ dl. milk	⅔ cup milk
2 eggs	2 eggs
for glaze and topping	**for glaze and topping**
2 oz./50 g. castor sugar	¼ cup granulated sugar
2 tablespoons water	3 tablespoons water
1 oz./25 g. walnuts	¼ cup walnuts
1½ oz./40 g. glacé cherries	¼ cup candied cherries

Well grease two 1-lb./450-g. loaf pans. Sift the flour and salt into a bowl, add sugar, walnuts and dates. Gently heat malt and butter or margarine until the fat has melted. Pour into the centre of the flour mixture with the blended milk and eggs. Mix together to a smooth, soft dough. Turn into the two prepared loaf pans. Bake for 1 hour in a very moderate oven.

For glaze and topping
Heat sugar and water in a pan and boil for 2–3 minutes until syrupy. When the loaves are cooked, turn out on to a wire rack and brush tops at once with glaze; decorate with nuts and cherries.

Nutty Orange Bread

Cooking time 1 hour
Oven temperature
350°F., 180°C., Gas Mark 4
Makes 1 loaf

Imperial/Metric	American
12 oz./350 g. self-raising flour	3 cups all-purpose flour, sifted with 3 teaspoons double-acting baking powder
½ teaspoon salt	½ teaspoon salt
3 oz./75 g. castor sugar	6 tablespoons granulated sugar
1½ oz./40 g. walnuts, coarsely chopped	good ¼ cup coarsely chopped walnuts
2 oz./50 g. candied orange peel, finely chopped	⅓ cup finely chopped candied orange peel
2 medium eggs, well beaten	2 eggs, well beaten
8–9 tablespoons (scant 3 dl.) cold milk	good 1 cup cold milk
2 oz./50 g. butter or margarine, melted	¼ cup melted butter or margarine
for glaze	**for glaze**
1 tablespoon castor sugar	1 tablespoon granulated sugar
1 tablespoon milk	1 tablespoon milk

Grease a 2-lb./1-kg. loaf pan. Sift the flour and salt into a bowl then stir in sugar, walnuts and peel. Mix to a slack consistency with the eggs and milk, stirring well. Fold in the melted fat, then turn mixture into prepared pan. Bake in the centre of moderate oven for 1 hour. Turn out on to a wire tray and brush top immediately with glaze.

Cut into slices when cold and serve with whipped cream and chunky strawberry jam.

For glaze
Put sugar and milk into a pan, heat until sugar dissolves then boil briskly for 3 minutes or until syrupy.

Glazed Cherry Bread

Nutty Orange Bread

Wholewheat Scones

Cooking time 10–15 minutes
Oven temperature
425°F., 220°C., Gas Mark 7
Makes 12 scones

Imperial/Metric	American
4 oz./110 g. plain flour	1 cup all-purpose flour
1 teaspoon baking powder	1 teaspoon double-acting baking powder
1 teaspoon salt	1 teaspoon salt
4 oz./110 g. wholewheat flour	1 cup wholewheat flour
2 oz./50 g. butter, margarine or cooking fat	¼ cup butter, margarine or shortening
2 teaspoons sugar	2 teaspoons sugar
approx. ¼ pint/1½ dl. milk	approx. ⅔ cup milk
milk to glaze	milk to glaze

Lightly flour a baking sheet. Sift plain flour, baking powder and salt together. Stir in wholewheat flour. Rub in fat finely. Stir in sugar, mix to a soft dough with milk. Knead lightly, then roll out on a floured board and cut into rounds with a plain pastry cutter. Place on prepared baking sheet, brush tops with milk. Bake near top of a hot oven for 10–15 minutes until risen. Cool on a wire rack.

Butterscotch Scones

Cooking time 15–20 minutes
Oven temperature
450°F., 230°C., Gas Mark 8
Makes 8 scones

Imperial/Metric	American
12 oz./350 g. self-raising flour	3 cups all-purpose flour, sifted with 3 teaspoons double-acting baking powder
2 oz./50 g. butter	¼ cup butter
1 oz./25 g. castor sugar	¼ cup granulated sugar
grated rind of 1 orange	grated rind of 1 orange
1 egg	1 egg
about 6 tablespoons milk	about ½ cup milk
2 heaped tablespoons orange marmalade	4 tablespoons orange marmalade
2 oz./50 g. currants	⅓ cup currants
for topping	**for topping**
1 oz./25 g. melted butter	2 tablespoons melted butter
1 oz./25 g. brown sugar	2 tablespoons brown sugar

Sift the flour, rub in the butter and stir in the castor sugar and orange rind. Add the beaten egg and milk, mixing to a soft but not sticky dough. Turn out on to a floured board, knead lightly to a smooth ball; roll to a rectangle about 12 inches by 9 inches (30 cm. by 23 cm.). Spread with marmalade, not quite to the edge, and sprinkle with currants. Roll up like a Swiss roll. Cut into thick slices.

For topping

Pour the melted butter into a shallow square or round cake pan, about 8 inches/20 cm. across. Butter sides and sprinkle bottom with brown sugar. Arrange scones in the pan, not quite touching each other. Bake in a very hot oven for 15–20 minutes.

Hunter's Rolls

Cooking time 15 minutes
Oven temperature
425°F., 220°C., Gas Mark 7
Makes 6 rolls

Imperial/Metric	American
6 oz./175 g. short crust or flaky pastry (see page 44)	6 oz. basic or rich flaky pie dough (see page 44)
for filling	**for filling**
4 oz./100 g. corned beef	¼ lb. corned beef
1 apple, peeled, cored and chopped	1 apple, pared, cored and chopped
2 teaspoons chopped pickled walnuts	2 teaspoons chopped pickled walnuts
2 teaspoons horseradish cream	2 teaspoons horseradish cream
beaten egg	beaten egg
salt and pepper	salt and pepper

Roll out pastry on a lightly floured board and cut into six pieces, 4 inches by 3 inches (10 cm. by 8 cm.). Finely chop the corned beef. Mix with apple, pickled walnuts and horseradish cream, bind with a little beaten egg. Season to taste. Roll the filling into six sausage shapes and place one on each piece of pastry, damp round pastry edges and roll up, press edges firmly together to seal. Place on a baking sheet and brush tops with beaten egg. Bake in a hot oven for about 15 minutes. Serve hot or cold.

Shown in colour on page 55

Christmas pudding, page 71

Marmalade Ring

Cooking time 45 minutes
Oven temperature
350°F., 180°C., Gas Mark 4
Makes 1 ring

Imperial/Metric	American
12 oz./350 g. self-raising flour	3 cups all-purpose flour, sifted with 3 teaspoons double-acting baking powder
3 oz./75 g. butter	6 tablespoons butter
3 oz./75 g. soft brown sugar	6 tablespoons brown sugar
2 oz./50 g. sultanas	⅓ cup seedless white raisins
1 standard egg	1 egg
¼ pint/1½ dl. milk, less 1 tablespoon	⅔ cup milk, less 1 tablespoon
3 level tablespoons coarsely cut orange marmalade	4 tablespoons coarsely cut orange marmalade
for icing	**for frosting**
2 tablespoons marmalade	3 tablespoons marmalade
2 oz./50 g. sieved icing sugar	½ cup sifted confectioners' sugar

Sieve the flour into a mixing bowl. Rub in butter until mixture resembles fine breadcrumbs. Stir in sugar and sultanas. Add the lightly beaten egg, milk and marmalade. Mix to a smooth dough. Shape dough into a 12-inch/30-cm. roll, then form into a ring.

Place ring on a greased baking sheet and bake in a moderate oven for 45 minutes. Allow to cool.

For icing

Gently heat the marmalade until hot, then stir in icing sugar. Pour icing over the baked ring.

Marmalade Ring

Ginger Nuts

Cooking time 15–20 minutes
Oven temperature
350°F., 180°C., Gas Mark 4
Makes 12 ginger nuts

Imperial/Metric	American
8 oz./225 g. plain flour	2 cups all-purpose flour
1 teaspoon bicarbonate of soda	1 teaspoon baking soda
1 teaspoon ground ginger	1 teaspoon ground ginger
2 oz./50 g. lard	¼ cup lard
2 oz./50 g. margarine	¼ cup margarine
3 oz./75 g. soft brown sugar	½ cup brown sugar, firmly packed
1 tablespoon golden syrup	1 tablespoon corn syrup
1 tablespoon lemon juice	1 tablespoon lemon juice

Grease two baking sheets. Sift the flour, soda and ginger together. Melt the fats in a saucepan (do not allow to boil), add the sugar, golden syrup and lemon juice and pour into the flour, mixing very thoroughly. Roll into balls about the size of a small walnut.

Place on prepared baking sheet, allowing a little room for spreading during cooking. Flatten each slightly with a damped finger. Bake in a moderate oven for 15–20 minutes. Leave to firm on the baking sheet for a few minutes before lifting on to a rack to cool.

Flapjacks

Cooking time 30 minutes
Oven temperature
325°F., 170°C., Gas Mark 3
Makes 12 flapjacks

Imperial/Metric	American
2 oz./50 g. margarine	¼ cup margarine
2 oz./50 g. sugar	¼ cup sugar
2 oz./50 g. black treacle	3 tablespoons dark molasses
2 oz./50 g. golden syrup	3 tablespoons corn syrup
4 oz./100 g. rolled oats	1 cup rolled oats

Melt the margarine in a pan with sugar, black treacle and golden syrup. When melted gently stir in the oats. Press into a Swiss roll pan.

Bake in a very moderate oven for 30 minutes. Mark into triangles while hot, leave in pan until cold, then remove separately.

Chocolate Brownies

Cooking time 30 minutes
Oven temperature
375°F., 190°C., Gas Mark 5
Makes 18 brownies

Imperial/Metric	American
4 oz./110 g. butter or margarine	½ cup butter or margarine
8 oz./225 g. soft brown sugar	1 cup brown sugar
2 eggs	2 eggs
4 oz./110 g. plain flour	1 cup all-purpose flour
1½ oz./40 g. cocoa powder	scant ½ cup cocoa
½ level teaspoon baking powder	½ teaspoon double-acting baking powder
good pinch of salt	good pinch of salt
for topping	**for topping**
castor sugar	granulated sugar

Grease a Swiss roll pan. Cream the butter and sugar together until light and fluffy. Add eggs, one at a time, beating thoroughly after each addition. Sift together the flour, cocoa powder, baking powder and salt. Stir into creamed mixture until well blended. Spread mixture in prepared pan.

Bake in a moderately hot oven for about 30 minutes, until firm to the touch in centre. Sprinkle with castor sugar while hot and cut in squares while still warm.

Walnut and Date Cookies

Cooking time 10–12 minutes
Oven temperature
400°F., 200°C., Gas Mark 6
Makes about 16 cookies

Imperial/Metric	American
3 oz./75 g. self-raising flour	¾ cup all-purpose flour, sifted with 1 teaspoon double-acting baking powder
1 oz./25 g. fine semolina	3 tablespoons fine semolina
2 oz./50 g. butter or margarine	¼ cup butter or margarine
1½ oz./40 g. castor sugar	3 tablespoons granulated sugar
2 oz./50 g. chopped dates	½ cup chopped dates
1 oz./25 g. walnuts, finely chopped	¼ cup finely chopped walnuts
1 medium egg	1 egg

Well grease a baking tray. Sift the flour into a mixing bowl, add semolina and rub in the fat lightly. Add sugar and the finely chopped dates and walnuts. Mix to a stiff consistency with the well beaten egg. Pile large teaspoons of the mixture on prepared baking tray.

Bake towards the top in a hot oven for 10–12 minutes. Cool on a wire tray.

Melting Moments

Cooking time 15–20 minutes
Oven temperature
350°F., 180°C., Gas Mark 4
Makes 20 cakes

Imperial/Metric	American
4 oz./100 g. margarine	½ cup margarine
3 oz./75 g. castor sugar	6 tablespoons granulated sugar
½ beaten egg	½ beaten egg
5 oz./150 g. self-raising flour	1¼ cups all-purpose flour, sifted with good 1 teaspoon double-acting baking powder
just under ½ teaspoon vanilla essence	scant ½ teaspoon vanilla extract
1 oz./25 g. rolled oats	scant ⅓ cup rolled oats

Grease a baking tray. Cream the margarine with sugar until soft and fluffy. Stir in beaten egg. Fold in sifted flour. Add vanilla essence. Spread rolled oats on a board or greaseproof paper. Use a teaspoon to form the mixture into small balls and dip the tops in oats to coat. Arrange on prepared baking tray, allow spreading room.

Bake in a moderate oven for 15–20 minutes or until golden brown. Leave a half minute on tray, lift on to wire rack to cool.

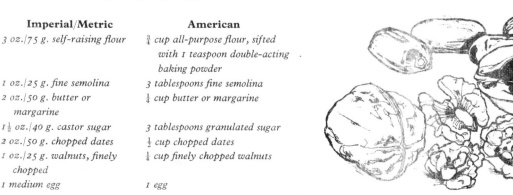

Golden Honey Cake

Cooking time about 1 hour
Oven temperature
350°F., 180°C., Gas Mark 4
Makes 1 cake

Imperial/Metric	American
4 oz./110 g. butter or margarine	½ cup butter or margarine
4 oz./110 g. castor sugar	½ cup granulated sugar
3 eggs	3 eggs
4 oz./110 g. (2 tablespoons) clear honey	3 tablespoons clear honey
8 oz./225 g. self-raising flour, sifted	2 cups all-purpose flour, sifted with 2 teaspoons double-acting baking powder
pinch of salt	pinch of salt
milk to moisten	milk to moisten

Line a greased 7-inch/18-cm. round cake pan with greased greaseproof paper. Cream the butter or margarine with castor sugar until light and fluffy. Gradually beat in the whisked eggs and the honey with a little of the sifted flour and a pinch of salt. Fold in the remaining sifted flour with sufficient milk to make a soft dropping consistency.

Turn into prepared pan and bake in centre of a moderate oven for about 1 hour, or until golden and cooked through. Cool and serve cut into slices. Spread with butter if desired.

Honey Sandwich

Cooking time 25–30 minutes
Oven temperature
350°F., 180°C., Gas Mark 4
Makes 1 cake

Imperial/Metric for sandwich cake	American for sandwich cake
6 oz./175 g. butter or margarine	¾ cup butter or margarine
4 oz./110 g. castor sugar	½ cup granulated sugar
1 tablespoon clear honey	good 1 tablespoon clear honey
3 eggs	3 large eggs
6 oz./175 g. self-raising flour	1½ cups all-purpose flour, sifted with 1½ teaspoons double-acting baking powder
pinch of salt	pinch of salt
2 tablespoons hot water	3 tablespoons hot water
sugar for dredging	sugar for dredging
for honey butter filling	**for honey butter filling**
4 oz./110 g. butter	½ cup butter
6 oz./175 g. icing sugar	1⅓ cups confectioners' sugar
2 tablespoons clear honey	3 tablespoons clear honey

Grease and line the base of two 7–8-inch/18–20-cm. sandwich cake pans with greased greaseproof paper. Cream the butter or margarine with the sugar and honey until really light and fluffy. Lightly whisk eggs and gradually beat into the creamed mixture. Carefully fold in sifted flour, salt and a little water. Divide mixture between prepared pans, smooth over tops with palette knife. Bake just above centre of a moderate oven for about 25–30 minutes or until golden brown and springy to the touch. Turn on to a wire rack to cool and strip off the paper. When quite cold sandwich together with the prepared honey butter filling and dredge the top well with castor sugar.

For honey butter filling

Cream the butter until very light and fluffy. Gradually beat in the sifted icing sugar until smooth and creamy, then stir in the honey until well blended.

Cherry Cake

Cooking time 1¼ hours
Oven temperature
350°F., 180°C., Gas Mark 4
Makes 1 cake

Imperial/Metric	American
4 oz./110 g. butter	½ cup butter
4 oz./110 g. castor sugar	½ cup granulated sugar
2 standard eggs	2 eggs
3 tablespoons milk	4 tablespoons milk
1 teaspoon grated lemon rind	1 teaspoon grated lemon rind
¼ teaspoon vanilla essence	¼ teaspoon vanilla extract
6 oz./175 g. plain flour	1½ cups all-purpose flour
pinch of salt	pinch of salt
1 level teaspoon baking powder	1 teaspoon double-acting baking powder
1 oz./25 g. ground almonds	¼ cup ground almonds
1 oz./25 g. semolina	3 tablespoons semolina
3 oz./75 g. glacé cherries, halved and quartered	⅓ cup candied cherries, halved and quartered

Line a greased 6-inch/15-cm. round cake pan with greased greaseproof paper. Cream the butter and sugar very well together, add the eggs gradually, beating between each addition. Scrape down the sides of the bowl, add the milk, lemon rind and vanilla essence and beat again to ensure even mixing.

Sieve the flour, salt and baking powder together, then with a metal spoon fold into the creamed mixture together with the almonds, semolina and cherries. Scrape down the sides of the bowl and fold again lightly. Put into prepared pan and bake on the middle shelf of a moderate oven for about 1¼ hours.

Roast duckling with orange and apple sauce, page 40

62

Victoria Sandwich

Cooking time 25–30 minutes
Oven temperature
350°F., 180°C., Gas Mark 4
Makes 1 cake

Imperial/Metric	American
4 oz./110 g. self-raising flour	1 cup all-purpose flour, sifted with 1 teaspoon double-acting baking powder
pinch of salt	pinch of salt
4 oz./110 g. butter or margarine, or mixture of both	½ cup butter or margarine, or mixture of both
4 oz./110 g. castor sugar	½ cup granulated sugar
2 standard eggs	2 eggs
approx. 2 tablespoons raspberry jam	approx. 3 tablespoons raspberry jam
2–3 teaspoons castor sugar for top	2–3 teaspoons powdered sugar for top

Grease two 6–7-inch/15–18-cm. sandwich cake pans. Sift flour and salt. Cream fat and sugar until light and fluffy, then beat in eggs, one at a time. Fold in flour with a metal spoon, then divide mixture equally between prepared pans, smoothing top of mixture. Bake in the centre of moderate oven for 25–30 minutes. Turn out and cool on a wire tray. When cold fill with jam and dust with castor sugar.

Spiced Raisin Cake

Cooking time 1¼ hours
Oven temperature
350°F., 180°C., Gas Mark 4
Makes 1 cake

Imperial/Metric	American
8 oz./225 g. butter	1 cup butter
6 oz./175 g. soft brown sugar	¾ cup brown sugar
2 tablespoons treacle	3 tablespoons molasses
2 eggs	2 eggs
10 oz./275 g. self-raising flour	2½ cups all-purpose flour, sifted with 2½ teaspoons double-acting baking powder
6 tablespoons milk	½ cup milk
for filling and topping	**for filling and topping**
2 oz./50 g. walnuts, chopped	½ cup chopped walnuts
1 oz./25 g. soft brown sugar	2 tablespoons brown sugar
1 level teaspoon powdered cinnamon	1 teaspoon powdered cinnamon
2 oz./50 g. seedless raisins, chopped	⅓ cup chopped seedless raisins

Mix the filling and topping ingredients together. Well grease a 7-inch by 11-inch (18-cm. by 28-cm.) ovenproof dish. Cream butter and sugar until light and fluffy. Blend treacle with eggs and gradually beat into creamed mixture. Fold in the flour and milk. Put half of mixture into prepared dish, cover with half of fruit and nut mixture. Add rest of cake mixture and top with remaining fruit and nut mixture.

Bake in a moderate oven for about 1 hour 15 minutes. Cut into squares and serve hot.

Rich Fruit Cake

Cooking time 2½–3 hours
Oven temperature
300°F., 150°C., Gas Mark 2
Makes 1 cake

Imperial/Metric	American
9 oz./250 g. plain flour	2¼ cups all-purpose flour
1 level teaspoon baking powder	1 teaspoon double-acting baking powder
pinch of salt	pinch of salt
8 oz./225 g. butter or margarine	1 cup butter or margarine
8 oz./225 g. castor sugar	1 cup granulated sugar
3 eggs	3 eggs
finely grated rind of 1 orange	finely grated rind of 1 orange
4 oz./100 g. each : cleaned currants, sultanas, seedless raisins	¾ cup each : cleaned currants, seedless white raisins, seedless raisins
2 oz./50 g. chopped peel	⅓ cup chopped candied peel
2 oz./50 g. ground almonds	½ cup ground almonds
2 oz./50 g. glacé cherries, cut	¼ cup candied cherries, cut
1 tablespoon sherry or milk	1 tablespoon sherry or milk

Grease and line an 8-inch/20-cm. cake pan with greased greaseproof paper. Sift the flour with baking powder and salt. Cream the butter or margarine with the sugar until light and fluffy. Gradually beat in one egg at a time with a tablespoon of the sifted ingredients. Stir in the grated orange rind, the currants, sultanas, raisins, peel, almonds and cherries. Fold in the remaining flour mixture, then stir in the sherry or milk.

Turn into prepared pan and smooth over the top with a palette knife. Bake in the centre of a slow oven for 2½–3 hours or until golden brown and firm to touch. Cool for 30 minutes in pan, then turn out and cool on a wire rack, remove paper. Store in an airtight tin.

Cut and Come Again Cake

Cooking time 1½ hours, approx.
Oven temperature
350°F., 180°C., Gas Mark 4
Makes 1 cake

Imperial/Metric	American
1 lb./450 g. plain flour	*4 cups all-purpose flour*
1 level teaspoon salt	*1 teaspoon salt*
2 level teaspoons baking powder	*2 teaspoons double-acting baking powder*
2 level teaspoons mixed spice	*2 teaspoons mixed spices*
6 oz./175 g. butter or margarine	*¾ cup butter or margarine*
6 oz./175 g. castor sugar	*¾ cup granulated sugar*
4 oz./100 g. raisins	*¾ cup seedless raisins*
4 oz./100 g. currants	*¾ cup currants*
2 oz./50 g. glacé cherries, chopped	*¼ cup candied cherries*
2 eggs	*2 eggs*
1 oz./25 g. warmed golden syrup	*1 oz. warmed treacle or corn syrup*
½ pint/3 dl. milk	*1¼ cups milk*

Line an 8-inch/20-cm. round cake pan with greased greaseproof paper. Sift the flour, salt, baking powder and mixed spice together into a large bowl. Rub in fat lightly until mixture resembles fine breadcrumbs. Stir in sugar, cleaned raisins, currants and cherries.

Whisk together the eggs, golden syrup and most of the milk. Add to dry ingredients and mix to a soft consistency, beating well, adding remaining milk if necessary. Turn into prepared pan. Bake on shelf below centre in a moderate oven for approximately 1½ hours, or until well risen and cooked through. Cool, remove paper and store in an airtight tin.

Old-English Cider Cake

Cooking time 45–50 minutes
Oven temperature
325°F., 170°C., Gas Mark 3
Makes 1 cake

Imperial/Metric	American
8 oz./225 g. plain flour	*2 cups all-purpose flour*
pinch of nutmeg	*pinch of nutmeg*
½ level teaspoon ground ginger	*½ teaspoon ground ginger*
½ level teaspoon bicarbonate of soda	*½ teaspoon baking soda*
4 oz./110 g. butter or margarine	*½ cup butter or margarine*
4 oz./110 g. castor sugar	*½ cup granulated sugar*
2 eggs	*2 eggs*
¼ pint/1½ dl. cider	*⅔ cup cider*

Grease a shallow baking pan about 8 inches by 6 inches (20 cm. by 15 cm.), with sloping sides. Sift the dry ingredients. Cream the butter and sugar until light. Beat in the eggs, one at a time. Stir in half the flour. Whisk the cider until frothy, then stir into mixture. Fold in remaining flour. Place mixture in prepared pan. Bang pan gently to settle mixture.

Bake in centre of a very moderate oven for 45–50 minutes. Leave one day before cutting.

Sticky Gingerbread

Cooking time 40–50 minutes
Oven temperature
350°F., 180°C., Gas Mark 4
Makes 1 cake

Imperial/Metric	American
12 oz./350 g. plain flour	*3 cups all-purpose flour*
pinch of salt	*pinch of salt*
1½ level teaspoons mixed spice	*1½ teaspoons mixed spices*
4½ level teaspoons ground ginger	*5 teaspoons ground ginger*
2½ oz./65 g. demerara sugar	*5 tablespoons raw sugar*
2½ oz./65 g. sultanas	*½ cup seedless white raisins*
6 oz./175 g. butter or margarine	*¾ cup butter or margarine*
3 tablespoons golden syrup	*4 tablespoons corn syrup*
3 tablespoons black treacle	*4 tablespoons molasses*
1½ level teaspoons bicarbonate of soda	*1½ teaspoons baking soda*
7 fl. oz./2 dl. warm milk	*scant 1 cup warm milk*
1 beaten egg	*1 beaten egg*

Grease and line a 7-inch/18-cm. square pan with greased greaseproof paper. Sift the flour, salt and spices into a mixing bowl. Stir in demerara sugar and sultanas. Place fat together with the syrup and treacle in a saucepan. Stir over a gentle heat until melted. Add to the dry ingredients and beat well. Dissolve bicarbonate of soda in the warm milk and add beaten egg. Pour this into the prepared mixture and beat well to form a smooth batter. Pour into the prepared pan.

Bake on centre shelf of a moderate oven for 40–50 minutes until well risen and springy to the touch. Cool slightly in pan, then turn on to wire rack, remove paper.

Note

Store in airtight tin for 2–3 days before use.

The Country Hostess

Entertaining is an important part of country life and a well-spread table the aim of every housewife worth her salt. She specially excels herself at the festivals of the year, like Christmas time. But the problems of dinner-party giving are the same in town or country. Here are a few tips to help you be a happy hostess:

Never try out a new dish for the first time on 'the night' – practise it first.

Write out a timetable to act as a working guide.

Have a definite colour scheme for the table setting; blend china, napkins, flowers and candles. Set the table in the morning.

For lavish effect serve food on large platters for guests to help themselves.

Follow recipes carefully – don't take short cuts, they may land you in trouble.

Cover dishes of hot food tightly with kitchen foil and put in a warm place to keep hot.

To keep gravy or sauce hot without it sticking to saucepan, stand it in a meat pan half-filled with simmering water in the oven. Cover the top of the sauce with wetted greaseproof paper to prevent a skin forming.

Make sure you've got kitchen foil, a bottle opener, a really sharp kitchen knife, plenty of dried herbs and simple things like salt, pepper and mustard.

Meal Starters

Mushroom Soup

Cooking time about 1 hour
Serves 4

Imperial/Metric	American
8 oz./225 g. mushrooms	*2 cups mushrooms*
1 chopped onion	*1 chopped onion*
1 oz./25 g. butter	*2 tablespoons butter*
1 pint/6 dl. stock	*2½ cups stock*
1 oz./25 g. flour	*¼ cup flour*
¾ pint/4 dl. milk	*good 1¾ cups milk*
salt and pepper	*salt and pepper*
4 tablespoons single cream	*5 tablespoons coffee cream*

Wipe and finely slice the mushrooms, chop the onion. Melt the butter in a saucepan and sauté the mushrooms and onion for 2–3 minutes until soft. Add the stock. Blend the flour with a little of the milk and add gradually to the soup with the rest of the milk.

Season to taste. Bring to the boil stirring all the while

and simmer for 45 minutes to 1 hour. Add the cream before serving but do not allow to boil.

Celery and Herb Soup

Cooking time 1 hour 10 minutes
Serves 4

Imperial/Metric	American
1 head of celery, washed and chopped	1 head (bunch) of celery, washed and chopped
1 onion, sliced	1 onion, sliced
1 carrot, sliced	1 carrot, sliced
1 oz./25 g. butter	2 tablespoons butter
¾ pint/4 dl. stock	1¾ cups stock
pinch of thyme	pinch of thyme
1 bay leaf	1 bay leaf
1 teaspoon chopped parsley	1 teaspoon chopped parsley
salt and pepper	salt and pepper
1 oz./25 g. flour	¼ cup flour
¾ pint/4 dl. milk	1¾ cups milk

Sauté prepared vegetables very gently in the melted butter in a pan for 5 minutes. Add stock, herbs and seasoning. Bring to the boil and simmer for 1 hour until vegetables are soft. Sieve the soup or put in a liquidiser. Blend the flour with a little milk, add with the rest of the milk to the soup. Bring to the boil and cook for 2–3 minutes. Garnish with chopped fresh herbs, if liked.

Pear Appetisers

Serves 4

Imperial/Metric	American
4 ripe pears	4 ripe pears
lemon juice	lemon juice
4 oz./100 g. cream cheese	¼ lb. cream cheese
4 teaspoons mayonnaise or salad cream	4 teaspoons mayonnaise or boiled salad dressing
4 tablespoons thick cream	5 tablespoons whipping cream
salt and pepper	salt and pepper
4 teaspoons chopped parsley	4 teaspoons chopped parsley
4 oz./100 g. ham, sliced and chopped	¼ lb. ham, sliced and chopped
lettuce	lettuce

Peel the pears, slice in half and remove cores. Dip the pear halves in lemon juice to preserve colour. Mix together the cream cheese, mayonnaise, cream and seasoning. Fold the chopped parsley and ham into the mixture. Pile mixture on to pear halves, and arrange two pear halves per person on lettuce on individual dishes.

Grapefruit Cups

Serves 4

Imperial/Metric	American
2 grapefruit	2 grapefruit
2 oz./50 g. castor sugar	4 tablespoons granulated sugar
2 oranges	2 oranges
2 dessert apples, cored and sliced	2 dessert apples, cored and sliced
4 maraschino cherries	4 maraschino cherries

Halve the grapefruit, remove segments and chop the fruit, flute edges of the grapefruit cups. Arrange the fruit in the base of the grapefruit cups and dredge with castor sugar. Peel the oranges and divide into segments. Arrange orange segments and apple slices on chopped grapefruit. Dredge with castor sugar. Decorate with cherries and serve chilled.

Summer Pâté

Cooking time 10 minutes
Serves 4

Imperial/Metric	American
4 oz./100 g. soft herring roes	¼ lb. soft herring roe
salt and pepper	salt and pepper
3 oz./75 g. butter	6 tablespoons butter
2 teaspoons lemon juice	2 teaspoons lemon juice
2 teaspoons chopped parsley	2 teaspoons chopped parsley

Season the roes with salt and pepper and gently fry in a little butter for 10 minutes. Pound to a fine paste with a wooden spoon. Soften the rest of the butter, add to roe paste. Add lemon juice and parsley. Serve with Melba toast or brown bread and butter.

Bacon Toasts

Cooking time 10 minutes
Serves 4

Imperial/Metric	American
4 slices bread	4 slices bread
butter	butter
4 tomatoes, sliced	4 tomatoes, sliced
4 slices Cheddar cheese	4 slices Cheddar cheese
4 rashers bacon, rinds removed	4 bacon slices

Toast the bread slices lightly on both sides. Remove crusts. Spread lightly with butter. Cover with a layer of tomato, and top with a slice of cheese. Cut bacon rashers in half and arrange on top of cheese. Grill until the cheese melts and turns golden, and the bacon is crisp.

Main Course Specials

Pineapple Gammon Steaks

Cooking time about 20 minutes
Serves 2

Imperial/Metric	American
2 gammon steaks	2 slices smoked ham, butt slices about ½ inch thick
1 × 16-oz./450-g. can pineapple rings	1 × 16-oz. can pineapple rings
3 tablespoons golden syrup or brown sugar	4 tablespoons corn syrup or brown sugar
watercress	water cress

Snip edges of the gammon steaks with scissors. Strain the juice from pineapple into a pan. Add gammon steaks. Cover with a plate, carrying the pineapple rings. Cover with foil or lid. Poach gently until tender, about 15 minutes.
Put steaks on a fireproof dish surrounded with pineapple. Cover all lightly with golden syrup or brown sugar. Place under hot grill for about 2 minutes. Serve pineapple on steaks topped with watercress. Pour a little of the liquor round each.

Savoury Bacon Pie

Cooking time 1¾ hours
Oven temperature
375°F., 190°C., Gas Mark 5
Serves 4

Imperial/Metric	American
2 sheep's kidneys	2 lamb kidneys
4 oz./100 g. mushrooms	1 cup mushrooms
1 oz./25 g. butter	2 tablespoons butter
6 rashers middle cut bacon	6 slices Canadian bacon
1½ lb./675 g. potatoes, peeled and sliced	1½ lb. potatoes, pared and sliced
4 oz./100 g. cheese, grated	1 cup grated Cheddar cheese
salt and pepper	salt and pepper
½ pint/3 dl. stock made with meat cube	1¼ cups stock, from a bouillon cube

Skin, core and quarter the kidneys. Quarter the mushrooms. Fry together 2 minutes in butter. Remove rind from bacon and cut two rashers into pieces. In a shallow casserole, place first a layer of sliced potato, then cheese, kidneys, mushrooms and chopped bacon, finishing with potatoes.
Arrange four rashers of bacon lengthwise, across top of casserole. Season stock, pour into casserole. Cover with lid or foil. Bake in the centre of a moderately hot oven for 1 hour. Remove lid. Continue baking for 30 to 45 minutes, until brown.

Honey-Baked Bacon

Cooking time about 1 hour
Oven temperature
375°F., 190°C., Gas Mark 5
Serves 4

Imperial/Metric	American
1¼ lb./550 g. middle or corner gammon	1¼-lb. piece smoked ham, center cut
1 bay leaf	1 bay leaf
pepper	pepper
1 small onion, skinned	1 small onion, skinned
2 tablespoons clear honey	3 tablespoons clear honey
½ teacup hot water	⅓ cup hot water

Leave the bacon to soak in cold water for 4 hours (or overnight). If packeted then follow instructions on label. Drain. Put into pan and cover with fresh water. Add the bay leaf, pepper and onion. Bring to the boil then simmer for 20 minutes per lb./450 g. or until tender. Drain and remove rind while joint is hot.

Put bacon in a meat pan. Mix honey with the hot water and pour over bacon. Cook for 30 minutes in moderately hot oven, basting twice during cooking.

Beef Terrine

Cooking time 1¼–1½ hours
Oven temperature
350°F., 180°C., Gas Mark 4
Makes 10 slices

Imperial/Metric	American
1½ lb./675 g. minced beef	1½ lb. ground beef
4 oz./100 g. pork sausage meat	¼ lb. pork sausage meat
2 level teaspoons made mustard	2 teaspoons prepared mustard
salt and pepper	salt and pepper
2 good pinches of dried tarragon (optional)	2 good pinches of dried tarragon (optional)
1 medium onion, chopped	1 medium onion, chopped
1 beaten egg	1 beaten egg
1 clove garlic, crushed	1 clove garlic, crushed
½ oz./15 g. butter	1 tablespoon butter
½ oz./15 g. plain flour	2 tablespoons flour
¼ pint/1½ dl. milk	⅔ cup milk
to garnish	**to garnish**
tomato wedges	tomato wedges
chopped parsley	chopped parsley

In a large bowl mix the minced beef, sausage meat, mustard, seasonings, tarragon, onion, egg and garlic. Make a thin white sauce in the usual way with the butter, flour and milk and blend into the meat mixture. Mix well until smooth. Grease a pâté or loaf pan and press the mixture in, smoothing the top. Cover with aluminium foil and cook in a moderate oven. Leave to cool. Turn out into a dish and remove any excess fat round the edges. Garnish with tomato wedges and chopped parsley. Serve sliced with mixed salad.

Jugged Hare with Forcemeat Balls

Cooking time about 3 hours 10 minutes
Oven temperature
325°F., 170°C., Gas Mark 3
Serves 4–6

Imperial/Metric	American
1 hare	1 hare
1–2 oz./25–50 g. dripping	2–4 tablespoons drippings
1 rasher bacon	1 bacon slice
1½ pints/1 litre stock or water	3¾ cups stock or water
1½ oz./40 g. flour, blended with a little stock	6 tablespoons flour, blended with a little stock
1 onion stuck with 2 cloves	1 onion stuck with 2 cloves
salt and pepper	salt and pepper
bouquet garni	bouquet garni
1 small bay leaf	1 small bay leaf
4 peppercorns	4 peppercorns
a small blade of mace	a small blade of, or ½ teaspoon, mace
2 teaspoons redcurrant jelly	2 teaspoons red currant jelly
1 glass of port or other type of red wine	1 glass of port or other type of red wine
for forcemeat balls	**for forcemeat balls**
4 oz./100 g. fresh white breadcrumbs	2 cups soft fresh bread crumbs
2 oz./50 g. shredded suet	⅓ cup finely chopped beef suet
2 teaspoons chopped parsley	2 teaspoons chopped parsley
a little grated lemon rind	a little grated lemon rind
1 teaspoon chopped thyme	1 teaspoon chopped thyme
a squeeze of lemon juice	a squeeze of lemon juice
salt and pepper	salt and pepper
beaten egg to bind	beaten egg to bind
1 tablespoon flour	1 tablespoon flour
fat for frying	fat for frying

Skin and paunch the hare, reserving the blood. Wipe the hare and cut into joints. Heat the dripping in a saucepan or flameproof casserole and fry joints in it with the chopped bacon. When the meat is lightly browned, add stock to cover, stir in the blended flour, the onion, seasoning and herbs, etc. Cover and cook very gently on top of cooker or in a very moderate oven for about 3 hours, or until tender. A few minutes before serving, remove the onion and bunch of herbs. Stir in the strained blood, redcurrant jelly and wine. Reheat without boiling. Garnish with cooked forcemeat balls.

To make forcemeat balls

Mix together the breadcrumbs, suet, parsley, lemon rind, thyme, lemon juice and seasoning. Add sufficient beaten egg to bind. Form into small balls and toss in flour to coat. Fry in hot fat, turning until golden brown and cooked through, about 10 minutes.

Roast Goose with Sage and Onion Stuffing

Cooking time about 4–5 hours, according to size
Oven temperature
400°F., 200°C., Gas Mark 6 for 15 minutes
350°F., 180°C., Gas Mark 4 for remainder of cooking time
Serves 6–8

Imperial/Metric	American
10–12 lb./4½–5½ kg. dressed goose	10–12 lb. goose, ready prepared
4 lemons	4 lemons
salt and freshly ground black pepper	salt and freshly milled black pepper
parsley	parsley
for sage and onion stuffing	**for sage and onion stuffing**
1½ lb./675 g. onions	1½ lb. onions
3 oz./75 g. butter	6 tablespoons butter
4 level teaspoons dried sage	4 teaspoons dried sage
8 oz./225 g. white breadcrumbs	4 cups fresh soft bread crumbs
salt and freshly ground black pepper to taste	salt and freshly milled black pepper to taste
1 egg	1 egg

Wipe the goose well inside and out with a clean damp cloth. Place prepared stuffing in neck end of goose, wrap flap over and secure with a small skewer. Weigh bird and calculate the cooking time, allowing 25 minutes per lb./450 g. Cut two lemons in half, place inside goose. Place goose in meat pan, rub seasoning over skin. Pour strained lemon juice from remaining lemons over. Do not add any fat as goose is sufficiently fatty. Cook goose in a hot oven for 15 minutes. Reduce heat to moderate and cook for remaining time until tender. Carefully transfer goose to serving dish, garnish with parsley.

For sage and onion stuffing

Peel and finely chop onions. Cook in 2 oz./50 g. melted butter for 5 minutes. Place in a bowl, add sage, breadcrumbs and seasoning. Bind together with remaining melted butter and lightly beaten egg.

Roast Turkey with Chestnut Stuffing and Accompaniments

Cooking time 3 hours 20 minutes–4 hours
Oven temperature
325°F., 170°C., Gas Mark 3
425°F., 220°C., Gas Mark 7 for last 30 minutes
Serves 8

Imperial/Metric	American
10–12-lb./4½–5½-kg. dressed turkey	10–12-lb. ready prepared turkey
salt	salt
4 oz./100 g. butter, softened	½ cup softened butter
2 oz./50 g. fat bacon	2 oz. salt pork
8 oz./225 g. streaky bacon	½ lb. bacon slices
1 lb./450 g. chipolata sausages	1 lb. chipolata or little pork sausages
for chestnut stuffing	**for chestnut stuffing**
1 lb./450 g. chestnuts	1 lb. chestnuts
½ pint/3 dl. milk and water mixed	1¼ cups milk and water mixed
4 oz./100 g. white breadcrumbs	2 cups fresh soft bread crumbs
2 oz./50 g. sausage meat	2 oz. sausage meat
1 level teaspoon mixed herbs	1 teaspoon mixed herbs
finely grated rind of 1 lemon	finely grated rind of 1 lemon
salt and freshly ground black pepper to taste	salt and freshly milled black pepper to taste
little beaten egg	little beaten egg

Wipe the turkey inside and out with a clean damp cloth. Place the prepared stuffing in neck end of the turkey. Wrap flap of skin over it and secure with a small skewer. Weigh turkey and calculate the cooking time, allowing 20 minutes per lb./450 g. Place turkey in meat pan, rub salt over skin then spread with butter.

Trim rind from fat bacon, place rashers over breast of bird. Cover closely with kitchen foil. Cook in a moderate oven for required cooking period. Meanwhile, trim rind from streaky bacon, flatten rashers with palette knife, roll up into neat rolls. Thread sausages and bacon rolls on to skewers. Thirty minutes before end of turkey cooking time, increase oven temperature to hot. Remove foil and fat bacon. Drain off most of the juices and fat, set aside for gravy. Place sausages and bacon rolls round turkey to cook. Replace in oven for 30 minutes. Transfer turkey to serving dish, arrange trimmings. Serve with gravy and bread sauce (see right).

For chestnut stuffing

Slit chestnuts on flat side and roast on a baking tray in a hot oven for 15 minutes. Peel off skins, keep chestnuts warm as they are more difficult to peel when cool. Put nuts on to boil in milk and water, reduce heat and simmer for 15 minutes until tender. Strain off liquid, reserve. Finely chop nuts or mince through a coarse-bladed mincer. Add remaining ingredients to nuts. Bind together with cooking liquid and beaten egg if necessary.

Gravy

Cooking time 5 minutes

Imperial/Metric	American
3–4 tablespoons dripping, and sediment from turkey fat	4–5 tablespoons drippings, and sediment from turkey fat
2 tablespoons flour	3 tablespoons flour
1 pint/6 dl. turkey stock, made from giblets	2½ cups stock, made from turkey giblets
gravy browning	gravy coloring
salt and pepper	salt and pepper

Heat the dripping from turkey fat in a saucepan. Stir in the flour and gradually add stock made up to 1 pint/6 dl. with water if necessary. Bring to the boil and cook for 3–4 minutes. Add a few drops of browning to make a rich colour. Season to taste.

Bread Sauce

Cooking time 10 minutes

Imperial/Metric	American
¾ pint/4 dl. milk	scant 2 cups milk
1 onion, peeled	1 onion, peeled
3 cloves	3 cloves
1 bay leaf	1 bay leaf
3 oz./75 g. fresh white breadcrumbs	1½ cups fresh soft bread crumbs
1 oz./25 g. butter	2 tablespoons butter
seasoning	seasoning

Pour the milk into a saucepan and add the onion studded with cloves. Add the bay leaf. Heat gently to simmering point. Remove from heat and allow to stand for 1–2 hours. Strain the milk and return to pan. Add breadcrumbs, together with butter. Season to taste and heat slowly until the sauce is thick and creamy.

Roast Pheasant with Mushrooms

Cooking time about 1 hour 10 minutes
Oven temperature
425°F., 220°C., Gas Mark 7 for 10 minutes
400°F., 200°C., Gas Mark 6 for rest of cooking time
Serves 4

Imperial/Metric	American
2 pheasants, about 2½ lb./ 1¼ kg., dressed	2 pheasants, 2½ lb., ready prepared
8 oz./225 g. button mushrooms	2 cups button mushrooms
6 oz./175 g. unsalted butter	¾ cup sweet (unsalted) butter
salt and freshly ground black pepper	salt and freshly milled black pepper
4–6 rashers fat bacon	4–6 bacon slices

Wipe the pheasants inside and out with a clean damp cloth. Wipe mushrooms. Place about 1 tablespoon of mushrooms and 2 oz./50 g. butter, in pats, inside each bird. Place pheasants in a meat pan, sprinkle with salt and freshly ground black pepper. Trim rind from bacon rashers, arrange over breasts of birds. Cover with a thickly buttered piece of greaseproof paper.

Cook pheasants on centre shelf of a very hot oven for 10 minutes, then reduce oven to hot and continue cooking for about 1 hour or until pheasants are cooked. Ten minutes before end of cooking time, remove paper and bacon, and baste pheasants well with juices from pan. Return to the oven to brown.

Simmer rest of the mushrooms in remaining melted butter for 5 minutes until tender, season to taste. Transfer cooked pheasants to hot serving dish. Drain the cooked mushrooms, spoon round the pheasants.

Festive 'Afters'

Syllabub

Serves 6–8

Imperial/Metric	American
juice and grated zest of 1 large lemon	juice and grated zest of 1 large lemon
4 tablespoons sweet sherry	5 tablespoons sweet sherry
2 tablespoons brandy	3 tablespoons brandy
2 oz./50 g. castor sugar	¼ cup granulated sugar
½ pint/3 dl. double cream	1¼ cups whipping cream
4 ratafia biscuits	4 ratafias or macaroons

Put the lemon juice and grated zest, sherry, brandy and sugar in a bowl. Stir until the sugar has dissolved. Add the cream and whisk until mixture forms soft peaks. Spoon into individual glasses and serve chilled. Sprinkle with crushed ratafia biscuits.

Christmas Pudding

Cooking time 6–8 hours
2–3 hours re-steaming
Makes 2 puddings (each pudding makes 6–8 servings)

Imperial/Metric	American
1 lb./450 g. seedless raisins	2⅔ cups seedless raisins
8 oz./225 g. currants	1⅓ cups currants
8 oz./225 g. sultanas	1⅓ cups seedless white raisins
4 oz./100 g. chopped mixed peel	⅔ cup chopped mixed candied peel
1 oz./25 g. almonds, blanched and chopped	¼ cup almonds, blanched and chopped
6 oz./175 g. self-raising flour	1½ cups all-purpose flour, sifted with 1½ teaspoons double-acting baking powder
8 oz./225 g. shredded suet	2 cups finely chopped beef suet
6 oz./175 g. dark brown sugar	¾ cup dark brown sugar
8 oz./225 g. fresh white breadcrumbs	4 cups fresh soft bread crumbs
¼ teaspoon grated nutmeg	¼ teaspoon grated nutmeg
pinch of salt	pinch of salt
3 eggs, well beaten	3 eggs, well beaten
grated rind and juice of 1 lemon	grated rind and juice of 1 lemon
4–5 tablespoons rum	5–6 tablespoons rum
milk to mix	milk to mix

Well grease two medium sized pudding basins. Wash and dry fruits. Put all dry ingredients into a basin. Add eggs and lemon juice and mix well together. Add rum and enough milk to mix to a stiff dropping consistency. Mix very thoroughly, leave overnight if wished. Press mixture into prepared basins. Cover with two thicknesses greased greaseproof paper and pudding cloth, tie securely. Steam for 6–8 hours for each pudding.

Re-cover, re-steam for 2–3 hours before serving. Serve with brandy butter (see below).

Shown in colour on page 59

Brandy Butter

Imperial/Metric	American
4 oz./100 g. unsalted butter	½ cup sweet (unsalted) butter
4 oz./100 g. castor sugar	½ cup granulated sugar
3–4 tablespoons brandy	4–5 tablespoons brandy

Cream the butter and sugar until light and fluffy, then gradually beat in the brandy. Pile into a serving dish. Leave in a cool place to set.

Hallowe'en Pumpkin pie

Sherry Cream Trifle

Serves 6

Imperial/Metric	American
8 small sponge cakes	sufficient lady fingers to cover base of serving dish
2–3 tablespoons raspberry jam	3–4 tablespoons raspberry jam
3 tablespoons sherry	3–4 tablespoons sherry
2 oz./50 g. crushed ratafia biscuits	2 oz. crushed ratafias or macaroons
1 pint/6 dl. hot custard	2½ cups hot custard
½ pint/3 dl. double cream	1¼ cups whipping cream
1 oz./25 g. castor sugar	2 tablespoons granulated sugar
for decoration	**for decoration**
split blanched almonds	split blanched almonds
halved glacé cherries	halved candied cherries
angelica leaves	candied angelica (optional)

Split the sponge cakes and spread the halves with jam. Arrange in a glass dish, pour over the sherry and soak for 30 minutes. Sprinkle ratafia biscuits over soaked sponge cakes. Pour custard on top to coat, and leave until cold. Whisk cream until thick, fold in sugar. Spread cream evenly over top of custard. Decorate with almonds, cherries and angelica.

Strawberry Mousse

Serves 4–6

Imperial/Metric	American
1 lb./450 g. fresh strawberries	1 lb. fresh strawberries
juice of ½ lemon	juice of ½ lemon
3 oz./75 g. castor sugar	6 tablespoons granulated sugar
½ oz./15 g. powdered gelatine	½ oz. (2 envelopes) gelatin
4 tablespoons hot water	5 tablespoons hot water
½ pint/3 dl. single cream or evaporated milk	1¼ cups coffee cream or evaporated milk
2 egg whites	2 egg whites
strawberry colouring (optional)	strawberry coloring (optional)

Hull the strawberries; reserve a few for decoration. Sprinkle remainder with the lemon juice and sugar to taste. Leave to stand for a short while, then rub through a sieve to form a purée. Dissolve the gelatine in the water over a gentle heat, stir into the purée. Add the cream or evaporated milk and stir until well blended. Whisk the egg whites until stiff, then carefully fold into mixture. Add a few drops of strawberry colouring if liked. Pour into a glass serving bowl. Leave to set in a cool place for several hours. Decorate with remaining strawberries.

Hallowe'en Pumpkin Pie

Cooking time 35–40 minutes
Oven temperature
375°F., 190°C., Gas Mark 5
Serves 4–6

Imperial/Metric	American
12 oz./350 g. short crust pastry (see page 44)	¾ lb. basic pie dough (see page 44)
milk and castor sugar for topping	milk and powdered sugar for topping
for filling	**for filling**
1½ pints/1 litre strained, cooked pumpkin	3¾ cups strained, cooked pumpkin
2 lb./1 kg. cooking apples, peeled, cored and sliced	2 lb. cooking apples, pared, cored and sliced
8 oz./225 g. sugar	1 cup granulated sugar
½ teaspoon ground cinnamon	½ teaspoon powdered cinnamon
½ teaspoon grated nutmeg	½ teaspoon grated nutmeg
½ teaspoon ground ginger	½ teaspoon ground ginger
¼ teaspoon ground cloves	¼ teaspoon ground cloves

Combine the pumpkin, apples, sugar, cinnamon, nutmeg, ginger and cloves. Mix well and turn into a large pie dish. Cover with the rolled out pastry, flute the edges and decorate the top with pastry leaves. Brush with milk and bake in a moderately hot oven for 35–40 minutes, or until apples are tender and pastry is golden.

Serve hot, sprinkled with castor sugar.

Drinks

One important thing to remember about drinks: when cold they should be very cold and when hot, they should be very hot, not lukewarm.

Refrigerators and easily prepared ice cubes make it easy to chill summer drinks and wine cups, but mulled drinks and punches need rather more care. When boiling is indicated in recipes, care should be taken not to boil the liquid with the spirit or wine in it, only heat gently to just below boiling point.

Some wine merchants will now hire you complete wine mulling equipment so that your brew stays at the correct temperature. The old way was to warm it by inserting a red-hot poker.

Punch bowls can also be hired. But if you don't want to do this, then use large earthenware jugs or pretty-up your biggest mixing bowl with a wreath of garden greenery tied round the rim.

If you're using delicate glasses for hot drinks, then warm them through first or alternatively place a silver spoon in each before filling; this prevents cracking.

To frost glasses for wine cups
Lightly beat the white of an egg, dip the rims of the glasses in the egg and then in castor sugar. Set aside to dry and harden before use.

Cold Drinks

Orange Cooler

Serves 3

Imperial/Metric	American
¾ pint/4 dl. milk	scant 2 cups milk
¼ pint/1½ dl. orange squash	⅔ cup orange drink
whipped double cream	whipped cream
crystallised orange slices	crystallized orange slices

Whisk the milk and orange squash together. Pour into glasses and top with whipped cream. Garnish with crystallised orange slices.

Lemonade

Serves 6

Imperial/Metric	American
3 lemons	3 lemons
6–8 oz./175–225 g. sugar	¾–1 cup granulated sugar
1½ pints/1 litre boiling water	3¾ cups boiling water
ice	ice
twist of lemon	twist of lemon

Wipe the lemons and finely grate the rind. Place the rind in a bowl with sugar to taste and pour in the boiling water. Cover and stand until cool. Add the juice of the lemons and strain into a jug. Place ice and a twist of lemon in each glass and top up with lemonade.

Blackcurrant Whip

Serves 3

Imperial/Metric	American
4 tablespoons sieved blackcurrant jam or	5 tablespoons black currant jelly or
¼ pint/1½ dl. fresh blackcurrant purée	⅔ cup fresh black currant purée
1 pint/6 dl. milk	2½ cups milk
sugar to taste	sugar to taste
brickette or small carton ice cream	½ pint ice cream

Whisk the blackcurrant jam or purée into the milk. Add the sugar and chill well. Pour into glasses and top with ice cream.

Honey and Almond Shake

Serves 3

Imperial/Metric	American
1 tablespoon clear honey	good 1 tablespoon clear honey
1 oz./25 g. ground almonds	¼ cup ground almonds
1 pint/6 dl. milk	2½ cups milk
little green colouring (optional)	little green coloring (optional)
1 egg white	1 egg white
whipped double cream	whipped cream
chopped almonds	chopped almonds

Whisk the honey and ground almonds into the milk. Add colouring. Whisk the egg white stiffly and fold into the mixture. Pour into glasses and top with the whipped cream and chopped almonds.

Iced Coffee

Serves 3

Imperial/Metric	American
2 oz./50 g. sugar	¼ cup granulated sugar
¼ pint/1½ dl. hot strong coffee	⅔ cup hot strong coffee
¾ pint/4 dl. milk	scant 2 cups milk
brickette or small carton ice cream	½ pint ice cream
grated chocolate	grated chocolate

Dissolve the sugar in the coffee. Add the milk and chill well. Pour into glasses and top with ice cream and sprinkle with grated chocolate.

Apple and Orange Refresher

Serves 4–5

Imperial/Metric	American
1 lb./450 g. dessert apples, peeled, cored and chopped	1 lb. dessert apples, pared, cored and chopped
juice of 1 lemon and water to equal ⅓ pint/2 dl.	juice of 1 lemon and water to equal scant 1 cup
1 oz./25 g. sugar	2 tablespoons sugar
juice of 3 oranges	juice of 3 oranges
for garnish	**for garnish**
orange wedges	orange wedges

Simmer the apples in the lemon juice and water and sugar until just tender. Blend in a liquidiser until smooth, mix with orange juice. Chill thoroughly. Serve in tall, stemmed glasses, place an orange wedge on the side of each glass.

Indian Summer Cider

Serves 4

Imperial/Metric	American
4 level teaspoons castor sugar	4 teaspoons granulated sugar
½ pint/3 dl. freshly made medium strength Indian tea	1¼ cups freshly made medium strength Indian tea
½ pint/3 dl. cider	1¼ cups cider
crushed ice	crushed ice
4 lemon slices	4 lemon slices

Add the sugar to the tea, stir until dissolved. Combine with the cider. Chill. Cover the base of each glass with crushed ice. Fill with the tea and cider mixture. Add a slice of lemon to each.

Indian Summer Cider

Wine Cobbler

Approx. 14 servings

Imperial/Metric	American
few ice cubes	few ice cubes
1 lemon, thinly sliced	1 lemon, thinly sliced
few sprigs of mint	few sprigs of mint
few maraschino cherries	few maraschino cherries
1 bottle of white wine	1 bottle of white wine
4 tablespoons lime juice	5 tablespoons lime juice
1 pint/6 dl. soda water	2½ cups club soda (carbonated soda)

Put the ice cubes, lemon slices, mint sprigs and cherries in the bottom of a large glass bowl or punch bowl. Pour the wine over and add lime juice and soda water.

Pomagne Julep

Serves 1

Imperial/Metric	American
1 teaspoon sugar	1 teaspoon sugar
1 sprig of fresh mint	1 sprig of fresh mint
1 teaspoon lemon juice	1 teaspoon lemon juice
3 ice cubes or crushed ice	3 ice cubes or crushed ice
1 lemon slice	1 lemon slice
Pomagne cider	champagne cider

Put the sugar, mint and lemon juice into a tall tumbler. Stir briskly to bruise the mint and extract the flavour. Add the ice. Stand the lemon slice on rim of the glass. Two-thirds fill with Pomagne cider. Stir and serve.

Hot Drinks

Chocolate Nog

Serves 3

Imperial/Metric	American
2 egg whites	2 egg whites
2 teaspoons brown sugar	2 teaspoons brown sugar
2 teaspoons chocolate powder	2 teaspoons chocolate powder
1 pint/6 dl. milk	2½ cups milk
1 tablespoon brandy (optional)	1 tablespoon brandy (optional)

Whisk the egg whites. Add sugar and chocolate powder. Heat the milk and fold in egg white mixture. Add the brandy and serve immediately.

Egg Flip

Serves 1–2

Imperial/Metric	American
1 egg	1 egg
1 teaspoon sugar	1 teaspoon sugar
2 teaspoons sherry	2 teaspoons sherry
½ pint/3 dl. milk	1¼ cups milk

Beat together the egg, sugar and sherry. Warm the milk and add it to the mixture. Heat slowly but do not allow to boil.

Blackcurrant Soother

Serves 1

Imperial/Metric	American
2–3 tablespoons blackcurrant syrup	3–4 tablespoons black currant syrup
juice of ½ lemon	juice of ½ lemon
1 teaspoon clear honey	1 teaspoon clear honey
½ slice of lemon	½ slice of lemon

Measure the blackcurrant syrup into a heatproof glass beaker. Add the lemon juice and honey. Fill up with boiling water. Float the lemon slice on top.

Treacle Posset

Serves 3

Imperial/Metric	American
1 pint/6 dl. milk	2½ cups milk
2 tablespoons black treacle	3 tablespoons molasses
3 teaspoons double cream	3 teaspoons whipping cream
a little powdered cinammon	a little powdered cinnamon

Heat the milk and dissolve the treacle in it. When sufficiently hot, pour into cups and float double cream on top. Sprinkle with cinnamon.

Note

Cream will float if it is poured over the back of a cold spoon.

Gaelic Coffee

Serves 1

Imperial/Metric	American
2 lumps sugar	2–3 teaspoons sugar (to taste)
3 tablespoons Irish whiskey	¼ cup Irish whiskey
hot black coffee	hot black coffee
lightly whipped cream	lightly whipped cream

Warm a large glass for each guest. Place sugar in the glass. Pour in the whiskey. Add very hot coffee and stir. Dip a teaspoon in the coffee and hold it just above liquid level. Pour in the cream over the spoon so that it floats on top. The true flavour is obtained by drinking the hot coffee and whiskey through the cream.

minutes. Strain out the cloves and lemon slices and reheat gently. Pour into a warmed punch bowl or jug, and serve in glasses with handles for easy holding.

To serve

Place a cinnamon stick and piece of lemon in each glass.

Hot Toddy

Serves 1

Imperial/Metric	American
1 tablespoon clear honey	1 tablespoon clear honey
juice of ½ lemon	juice of ½ lemon
1 tablespoon whisky	1 tablespoon whisky
1 lemon slice	1 lemon slice

Put the honey, lemon juice and whisky into a heatproof tumbler or beaker. Fill up with boiling water and stir well. Float a slice of lemon on top. Serve very hot as a nightcap.

'Sweet Dreams' Nightcap

Serves 1

Imperial/Metric	American
½ pint/3 dl. warm milk	1¼ cups warm milk
2 teaspoons clear honey	2 teaspoons clear honey
2 teaspoons rum	2 teaspoons rum

Heat the milk and honey until almost boiling. Pour into a warmed glass. Stir in the rum. Drink at once.

Cider Honey Punch

Approx. 16 servings

Imperial/Metric	American
2 flagons cider	3 quarts cider
4 tablespoons thick honey	⅓ cup thick honey
1 level teaspoon powdered cinnamon	1 teaspoon powdered cinnamon
6 cloves	6 cloves
a good grating of nutmeg	a good grating of nutmeg
2 good pinches of ground ginger	2 good pinches of ground ginger
1 sliced lemon	1 sliced lemon
to serve	**to serve**
cinnamon sticks	cinnamon sticks
lemon slices	lemon slices

Heat all ingredients together slowly, except for the decoration, until hot and nearly boiling. Do not bring to the boil, but stir, cover and leave to infuse for 15

Mulled Wine

Serves 6–8

Imperial/Metric	American
1 bottle of inexpensive red wine	1 bottle of inexpensive red wine
3 tablespoons clear honey	4 tablespoons clear honey
good pinch of cinnamon	good pinch of cinnamon
1 orange studded with cloves	1 orange studded with cloves
¼–½ pint/1½–3 dl. boiling water	⅔–1¼ cups boiling water
3–4 tablespoons brandy	4–5 tablespoons brandy

Gently heat together the wine, honey, cinnamon and the orange. Stir well and do not allow to boil. Add boiling water and pour into punch bowl or large jug. Just before serving stir in the brandy.

Buttered Rum

Serves 1

Imperial/Metric	American
1 teaspoon castor sugar	1 teaspoon granulated sugar
2½ fl. oz./75 ml. boiling water	⅓ cup boiling water
2½ fl. oz./75 ml. rum	⅓ cup rum
pat of butter	pat of butter
grated nutmeg	grated nutmeg

Heat a tumbler or china mug, and put in the sugar. Add the water, rum and butter and stir. Sprinkle with grated nutmeg and serve at once.

Index

Acknowledgements

The author and publishers thank the following for
their co-operation in supplying
colour photographs for this book:
CEREBOS FOODS LIMITED
(distributors of Atora Shredded Beef Suet) page 59
FRUIT PRODUCERS' COUNCIL pages 19, 31, 51, 55
WHITE FISH AUTHORITY page 31
All black and white photographs are by courtesy of the
FLOUR ADVISORY BUREAU
except for the following:
H. P. BULMER LIMITED page 75
FRUIT PRODUCERS' COUNCIL pages 24, 38, 71
POTATO MARKETING BOARD pages 7, 12